Joyfully
In His
Care

JOYFULLY IN HIS CARE:
Women Living In All Circumstances

by
Women of Faith

Compiled and Edited by

Project HerStory
The Women's Ministry
First Baptist Church of Highland Park
Landover, Maryland

Published 2020 by First Baptist Church of Highland Park, 6801 Sheriff
Road, Landover, MD 20785; www.fbhp.org.

ISBN 978-1-7343446-0-8

Compiled and edited by Project HerStory of the Women's Ministry,
First Baptist Church of Highland Park.

Some names and identifying details have been changed to protect the
privacy of individuals.

Photography by Photography Ministry, First Baptist Church of Highland Park.

Cover design and interior layout by Eddie Egesi, 2019.

Excerpt from The Valley of Vision: A Collection of Puritan Prayers and
Devotions. Edited by Arthur Bennett, Banner of Truth, 1975.
Used by permission.

Printed by Color Marketing in the United States of America

DEDICATION

To women of all ages amid life seasons of drought and darkness, you are not forgotten. Trust God, have faith, and know He is always with you. His healing is on the way.

"Thou art preparing joy for me and me for joy;
I pray for joy, wait for joy, long for joy;
give me more than I can hold, desire, or think of.
Measure out to me my times and degrees of joy,
at my work, business, duties.
If I weep at night, give me joy in the morning."

~ Arthur Bennett, *The Valley of Vision*

CONTENTS

Chapter One - Contributors A through D

"But those who trust in the LORD will find new strength."
~ Isaiah 40:31

Chapter Two - Contributors E through K

"For I can do everything through Christ, who gives me strength."
~ Philippians 4:13

Chapter Three - Contributors L through R

"But Blessed are those who trust in the Lord and have made the Lord their hope and confidence." ~ Jeremiah 17:7

Table Of Contents

Chapter Four - Contributors S through W

"Thank you for making me so wonderfully complex!
Your workmanship is marvelous—how well I know it." ~ Psalm 139:14

FOREWORD

By Dr. Henry P. Davis III

Prayer has always been essential to the heart of the Black Church. This is not particular to persons of color. It is fundamental to the Christian faith, along with one's testimony. Anyone who has been in church since ages past can remember attending prayer meetings where there were as many testimonies as there were prayers. As young people, we could not grasp the significance of moments like these and would be found snickering about the stories we heard. But time changed all that as we started going through our own life experiences with disappointments along with miraculous victories. Situations such as walking away from automobiles that were totaled gave us a full appreciation that it only could have been the power and grace of God.

Testimonies are important in the Christian faith because they open a window into the core of one's very soul. Testimonies are not a script — they are faith statements that come directly out of the challenges, struggles, and victories in one's life. Every believer should have a personal testimony, or faith statement, to share with others. These faith statements can help others grow closer to the Lord and even accept Jesus Christ as Lord and Savior.

Sharing one's testimony is a sign of spiritual growth. Romans 15:1 states, *"We who are strong must be considerate of those who are sensitive about things like this. We must not just please ourselves."* Our faith cannot be selfish, as God places us here to be a blessing to others. It is easy to focus on one's inadequacies instead of embracing the reality that we serve a God

xiii

of purpose, Who does nothing by accident. He only operates in divine providence. One could think their story is unimportant, but they need to know God answered their prayers, brought them through, and now they can be a blessing to someone else.

Months ago, the idea came up at First Baptist Highland Park that women of our church should consider publishing their testimonies so that others would know how the hand of God moved in their lives. In the pages to follow, you will read some wonderful victory stories — joyous "hallelujahs" on the backside of hurt, praises out of pain, and affirmations about being victors and not victims. You will see how God can move in many ways. Some persons may want to keep their stories close to heart, but then they realize sharing has the potential for giving others a sense of release. These women of faith chose to share, and as a result, we can gain strength from them as we walk alongside living miracle stories.

The Word of God is so true when it tells us the importance of one's faith. Hebrews 11:1 states, *"Faith shows the reality of what we hope for; it is the evidence of things we cannot see."* Unfortunately, much of faith has been so commercialized. Many have strayed away from the very things that brought us to where we are. Suicide, a rising epidemic, has entered the doors of the church such that we read about faith leaders deciding this is the only alternative. Our collective prayer is these stories of faith will give persons hope, so they will not give up on themselves or the love of God.

We praise God that the First Baptist Church of Highland Park is a *Bible Believing, Christ Centered, and Spirit Led* congregation. We count it as a joy to share these faith stories with others. And, we pray without ceasing this work will enhance the reader and bless the Body of Christ.

PREFACE

By Rev. Goldie B. Walker

God would not permit the seed for this book of testimonies to die. After all, it was for His glory and not mine. It remained in the belly of my heart and soul for twenty years without germination – like an unwanted pregnancy planted by an unwanted lover but instead it was planted by the Holy Spirit, the lover of my soul. But a day is like a thousand years to the Lord, and a thousand years is like a day. This seed would remain in my womb undisturbed until its mission, church and God's handpicked contributors were in full season and ready to develop into His purpose and His use in the Kingdom of God.

The common thread that links together each testimony is the strengthened relationship and joy found resting in the Almighty God through the blood of Jesus which empowers each woman of faith to live a life of resolved satisfaction and peace in all circumstances. Thus, the heartbeat passage is 1 Thessalonians 5:16-18: *"Always be joyful. Never stop praying. Be thankful in all circumstances, for this is God's will for you who belong to Christ Jesus."* Hence, presented is the book entitled, *Joyfully In His Care: Women Living In All Circumstances.* It is meant to build up, encourage and plant seeds of faith, in the hearts of believers and unbelievers; and to show prototypes of overcomers to those in similar circumstances.

As a passionate reader and collector almost entirely of spiritual books, I became fascinated and intrigued with a book given to the Walker Family by my in-laws, Fred and Carrie Sanders. In the beginning, I was captivated by the title, *Miracles on Monroe Street* which caught my attention as a spin off from the 1947 movie, "Miracle on 34th Street."

Instead, the book was a collection of testimonies written by members of the Sanders' home church community, Celebration Church of God, located on Monroe Street in Baltimore, Maryland. As I perused the contents of the book, my heart pounded with the desire to have "my own book of testimonies" written by those in my circle of influence. However, God had a bigger plan all along. He flipped the script to press upon my spirit that "this book is not for your glory, but for *My* glory, and the book is to contain testimonies of women within your home church."

I cried out to the Lord that the assignment was a voluminous task and that I knew of no committed souls to assist me in composing, compiling, completing or even embarking upon, for me, uncharted territory. He has proven repeatedly over my life time, that as His chosen one, His presence shall go with me as He promised Moses in Exodus 33:14, Joshua in Joshua 1:5, and as Angel Gabriel said to Mary in Luke 1:37, *"For the word of God will never fail."*

Today, I believe and stand firmly on His Word as a reason for my own joyful living in His care. As a woman of God who has lived and continue to live in all circumstances, I am a recipient of His many unforeseen and faithful blessings. Some of my blessings occurred in His divine intervention in the early 70s and beyond when He protected me from becoming a rape victim; provided transportation home from night school when I sought my bachelor's degree; embodies me with good health without surgery; and opened doors for me when I was financially strapped.

Further, I'm blessed with a godly husband, Leon, of 38 years, who is my true champion, and an inactive trustee of our church and a retired senior partner of a CPA Firm. Since a stroke in 2011, we live with his limited and restricted mobility along with his other challenges. The mainstream of my daily living is driven by juggling and balancing the essentials and desires of both our care and necessities of life given by God to live godly.

These include obligations and commitments to a growing family (three wonderful children, five grandchildren and two great-grandchildren) and the multiple opportunities associated with church. God provides for all our needs, as He promises, during this season of our marriage which is continually on display as we thrive as believers, living in all circumstances, meeting every challenge head-on with holy boldness wherever we are, whether at the gym, shopping, travelling, in church, theater, restaurant, medical appointments or fellowship.

Others often tell us that our marriage serves as an inspiration; and to us, an assigned ministry from above. Daily we feel His lovingkindness in our lives and take notice of His abundant grace and miraculous power knowing that through strength in Christ, we can do all things. When we suffered a miscarriage, God was there; and He was there when we lost Lionel, our stillborn son during a difficult pregnancy.

I know that without the presence of God in my life, then and now, I would be a basket case. I am retired with 39 years from a government service career in finance and project management. I became the benefactor of shared family joy when Leon received a namesake award in March 2019 – The Leon Walker Pioneer Award – presented by his brothers in Kappa Alpha Psi Fraternity, Inc., The Hyattsville/Landover/MD Alumni Chapter.

Moreover, in the evening of March 20, 2006, after an overwhelming and exhausting day at work, the clear and distinct voice of the Holy Spirit came from the threshold of my bedroom door, where I lay resting, with seven words: "Jesus said God is depending on you." As I reflected on all my unaccomplished tasks, the book of testimonies blasted the loudest. Through God's equipping for ministry, I finished seminary in 2011. I received my license to preach July 23, 2014, where I serve amongst other capacities, as an associate minister in my home church, beloved First Baptist Church of Highland Park, Landover, Maryland and lead a weekly Bible lesson in my community. Confirmed spiritual ministries by the Spirit into my spirit of discernment, hospitality and public relations contribute to my call by God to spread the gospel of Jesus Christ.

I could go on and on about my own intimate reasons for making every attempt possible to remain unswerving in practicing to live this joyful season of favor -- truly accredited to the God I serve and His love shown me through the redeeming work of His Son, Jesus Christ. Did this mindset happen overnight? No. Only through purposeful self-examination and self-improvement under the inspiring encouragement of a compassionate and fulfilling God of hope and love, do I credit with a grateful heart for the desire to emulate Christ Jesus in continued growth and enduring strength. Am I perfect? By no means, but He is.

Through the joys, the trials and struggles of life, through faith by abundant grace and tender mercy I receive through knowing Christ, I am brought into a deeper and joyful fruit-producing and growing relationship with Jesus. And now, I know that at this juncture of my life, with tested faith, God waited for me to be still and to know without a doubt that He is the Author and Finisher of all things; including the assignment placed on my life to spearhead this publication. Therefore, rest assured that only God could deliver for your reading pleasure and spiritual enhancement an astounding product such as *Joyfully In His Care: Women Living In All Circumstances*.

As I surrender to God's plan, His provisions equip where I am ill-equipped. The pressure had increased now because God wanted the book of testimonies for His glory and my desire was to do my part to give Him the best outcome I could. He knew there would be challenges and setbacks; and He knew from the very beginning that if only one woman found relief in making her story a legacy and others were blessed from that experience, then the mission to glorify God had been accomplished. In addition, this publication depicts the true legacy contribution written in the voice of the respective writers and enables their future generations to know the faith believing journey of victorious living.

Therefore, God watches today as He watched in Jeremiah 1:12 to see that His work is fulfilled. For God promises that His word always produces fruit and it will accomplish all He wants it to, and that it will prosper everywhere He sends it. Now seventeen years after making First Baptist Church of Highland Park the home church of the Walker Family, God's plan for the book of testimonies resurfaces again in my heart. I knew my wilderness experience was about to end at the close of the 2014 Women's Prayer Conference. It was there that I uttered God's mission and vision for a book of testimonies with my Conference co-partner, Deacon Yvonne Lowe, a retired federal executive.

Then, I was privileged on occasion to serve as a part of the Good News Jail and Prison Ministry of the church and to bring the gospel to the women at the Upper Marlboro Correctional Facility with Dr. Tamara Henry, a professor at Towson University, who agreed to serve as chief editor. God manifested His command and my assignment through the combined supportive spirits with these two women among others noted in the Acknowledgments section of the book. As God set the stage, His process for the book of testimonies that He be glorified took flight in late 2018 with the initiation of Project HerStory.

I am grateful to each woman God appointed to answer the clarion call to share a story of overcoming difficulty in trying times, thereby cleansing the inner closets of her soul, and opening her heart to share events and experiences that once restrained her mouth closed. Through this publication, God's goodness, kindness and tender mercy illuminates. For these women of faith, their testimonies are much alike as they share that the secret to living joyfully in His care is having a Christ-centered approach to living in all circumstances. They understand that fundamental tools in the battle against spiritual warfare consist of a constant prayer life and a continuous study of God's Word, along with witnessing to others His deeds and gathering in worship and fellowship with those of like minds.

Existing joyfully in His care requires complete devotion and submission to the heavenly Father. Alternatively, by allowing the drywall in the closet of the inner self to collapse under the weight of abuse, doubt, depression, despair, confusion, fear, brokenness, rejection, loneliness and anxiety zaps one's self-esteem to live in God's presence and becomes a dream killer and a show stopper. It is by faith alone in Christ that these women have become new creations transformed from within and brought out of their corrupting trials to the outside world, enabling the light from above to control their lives and therefore enabling usefulness in the Kingdom of God. These women are winners walking in the newness of praise, worship, song, comedy, restoration of shattered hopes, and healing from financial, emotional, social and physical ailments.

Finally, I congratulate my sisters of *Joyfully In His Care: Women Living in All Circumstances* for their coming clean boldness on the issues shared in the true life testimonies of reflections you are about to read. I am grateful to each woman for their unknowing reassurance and encouragement to me when needed the most as I read repeatedly the words of each testimony. The divine providential plan of God is that these prearranged women be prepared to answer the clarion call to partake of the opportunity to tell others the reason they live joyfully in His care.

Therefore, it is not unusual that it took two decades for this book of testimonies to be birthed; God always has an unrevealed plan in motion as for Joseph. It is not unusual that at such a time as this, the debut of *Joyfully In His Care: Women Living In All Circumstances* aligns with the 2019 increased call for evangelism and missions in all church ministries at First Baptist Church of Highland Park, under the esteemed leadership of Dr. Henry P. Davis III. It is not unusual that God fulfills His promises through the Holy Spirit to those who hear, listen and act in faith by grace to receive mercy and forgiveness; trusting that God does not lie. After all, it took 42 generations before Jesus, the Savior of the world, would appear after the proclamation by Old Testament prophets of His coming.

May the presence of God be with the contributing authors and with you! Enjoy the read and be strengthened to live joyfully in His care alone. Shalom.

INTRODUCTION

What compels someone to share a personal story about a life-changing experience? Why would someone else want to read about that experience? How do lives change by knowledge of that experience? We contemplated these questions when the Project HerStory team, inspired by the Holy Spirit, formed and began our mission in 2018 to compile an extraordinary book of testimonies with real-life stories, by ordinary women of faith, that inspire, uplift, and empower every reader, and most of all, glorify God.

The Project HerStory team encouraged potential contributors to write testimonies about encounters with God that had a memorable impact on their lives — and write they did. As stories came in from contributors as young as seventeen, matriarchs in their nineties, and women of all ages in between, we knew *Joyfully In His Care: Women Living In All Circumstances* would be special. Reading about their journeys, with life's unexpected twists and turns that tested and strengthened their faith, truly strengthened our faith in the Most High God and His Son, our Lord and Savior Jesus Christ. We read these testimonies many times over while compiling and preparing them for publication. The impact on our thoughts, hearts, and minds was unmistakable — we desired to be better women, better Christians, and better citizens in the Kingdom of God. We rejoiced, prayed, and praised God for His faithfulness. Most of all, we wanted these testimonies available worldwide that they may be a testament of the goodness, mercy, and enduring love of the Almighty God.

We organized the testimonies, alphabetically by names of the authors, across four chapters. We thought this approach allows readers to encounter them as we did — randomly without preconceived notions of what we were about to read. Ultimately, we used this approach with hopes of positioning readers for receiving revelations and affirmations about life as a Christian, and perhaps, a charge to draw closer to God.

We prepared this book for all readers — women and men; teens and tweens; and Christians and non-Christians. We prepared it for reading over and over again. Nuggets of wisdom about living a joyful life, no matter the circumstances, can be discovered with each reading.

Lastly, we thought it fitting to end the book by featuring the courageous Women of Faith, whose life stories grace the pages of this book. We believed readers, as they consume the stories, will want to know more about these women, and even see them, if possible. So, we added the "About the Contributors" section with short biographies and photos to satisfy this desire.

~ The Project HerStory Team

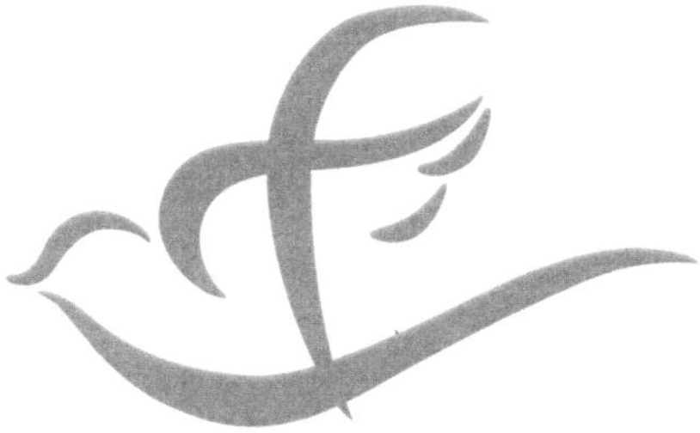

"Have you never heard?
Have you never understood?
The LORD is the everlasting God
the Creator of all the earth.
He never grows weak or weary.
No one can measure the depths of his understanding.
He gives power to the weak
and strength to the powerless.
Even youths will become weak and tired,
and young men will fall in exhaustion.
But those who trust in the LORD will find new strength.
They will soar high on wings like eagles.
They will run and not grow weary.
They will walk and not faint."

~ Isaiah 40:28-31

Chapter One

Contributors A through D

"But those who trust in the LORD

will find new strength."

~ Isaiah 40:31

FINDING THE GOD OF MY UNDERSTANDING

By Victorine Adams

It was 8 p.m. on February 5, 2015, when I got into a heated argument with my boyfriend who later became my husband. We had been in Prince George's County for 11 years, living on the streets and in abandoned houses in the Landover, Maryland area. On this date, we were living on Kent Village Drive and used the nearby Exxon Gas station to wash up or to get water to prepare food. We lived under these conditions, not worrying about our next meal. We were in our own world living ungodly.

For many years, I had lost all hope. Many times I prayed and asked God to change things for the better. I prayed that He would bring us closer to Him. Then, there were times I wanted to give up because I felt my life wasn't what I would have liked it to be. While I knew how to pray, I never picked up a Bible to read.

The night I got into the argument, I decided to take a walk. I walked down the street to Martin Luther King Jr. Highway to a liquor store and talked with a few friends.

Afterwards, I walked back up Columbia Park Road and stood there talking with another friend who had walked me to that corner on Kent Village Drive. While talking, I saw my boyfriend come to the door of the abandoned apartment for a few seconds, and then go back inside.

I ended my conversation, crossed the street and turned up into the driveway when I saw someone standing in the dark under the bathroom window. As I got closer, I was shot point blank in the left eye. An ambulance rushed me first to Prince George's Hospital Center in Cheverly, Maryland to be stabilized and later took me to the University of Maryland Medical Center's shock trauma unit in Baltimore. I stayed there one month.

It was during my hospital stay in Baltimore that I found a power greater than me. I found my faith in God and began to talk to Him like I never had talked to anyone before. I prayed and talked to God like He was right there in the room. I now know He was. Although I could not physically talk, I was speaking from my heart, building a relationship with the God of my understanding. As these days of prayer and meditation continued, God started moving in my life, opening doors and moving mountains that only He can move. If it wasn't for the God of my understanding, I don't know where I would be today.

By March 2015, I was up feeding myself and praising God on a regular basis. Nothing could stop me now. I had a personal relationship with God. I was growing in faith and began to develop plans for my life. My first mission was to join First Baptist Church of Highland Park in Landover, Maryland. I wanted to get involved, so I joined the church's liturgical dance ministry, Praise Power. Then, I found stable housing. Finally, I enrolled at Prince George's Community College.

I survived my fourth brain surgery on October 4, 2018. Here I still stand, growing stronger in the knowledge of the God of my understanding.

AN OPEN LETTER TO SERVANTS OF GOD:

He Blesses Us To Be A Blessing To Others

By Cynthia Faye Alexander

Now, thinking back on the many times Almighty God provided loving care and protection for me and my three children, I realize we received His blessings because He is God. I didn't really ask for blessings because I never knew to ask. He knew what we needed and provided it. As a twice-divorced, single parent of one boy and two girls who are 11 years apart in age, I needed Him and didn't know it; but, praise God, He blessed me and my children over and over again. There were times I just wanted to go someplace, anywhere, far away from things that were happening in my life. God was there for me, even though I didn't think of it that way at the time.

My family and I lived in a large home in Wheaton, Maryland. However, for a while, following a separation and an eventual divorce, my children and I lived in locations around Maryland and Southeast, Washington, D.C. Over time, savings from job earnings and proceeds from the sale of the house in Wheaton allowed me to purchase a condo in Landover – nearer to my parents, two brothers, four sisters, and three cousins. Just look at God! Although the condo was smaller than the house in Wheaton and other places we'd lived, the move was a good one for me and my children because of the close relationships we developed with my parents, siblings, and cousins. In fact, closer family relationships made a big difference for all of us. I really missed the space we had in the Wheaton home, but not the work involved in taking care of it. I give God all the glory and praise for being able to do more and have more, with what I thought was less.

God always knows just what we need and truly helps us in ways that we don't appreciate until later in our journey. When I was in my teens and early 20s, I thought I didn't need God. I didn't know how to depend on Him. When you are young, you don't think! I thought I was okay because I had good jobs but, being a single parent was hard. I wanted to do better but didn't know how. Now that I'm a great grandmother and have established a close relationship with God and His Son Jesus, I often think about the many times I missed doing and giving what I could to be a blessing to my family.

It shames me when I think of the many times that I did nothing at all and often felt completely like nothing. This behavior disappoints God and saddens me as I think about it. I can never get that time back. I wish I had done more.

Now, I say, "we must do all we can while we can because we don't know when we won't be able to do anything at all." I don't take anything for granted anymore.

Even as I age and feel as though I can't move or talk the way I use to, I must do what I can to be a blessing to others. How? Praying and studying God's Word can help. Doing this truly has helped me to be a better servant of God. I look forward to seeing and hearing Him say, "Well done, My servant. Come join Me at home, a place prepared for you."

Also, asking and waiting for God's aid in all that we do and say will allow Him to bless us so that we can be a blessing to others. When I meditate on how I may serve as God would have me to serve, I look at *"Let the words of my mouth, and the meditation of my heart, be acceptable in thy sight, O Lord, my strength, and my redeemer."* (Psalm 19:14 KJV)

HUMBLE BEGINNINGS ...BUT GOD!

By Shirley K. Ballard

It is with great pleasure that I write to share childhood experiences that haunted me over the years but became reality as I grew into adulthood. I grew up in rural Virginia, in a town near the Rappahannock River that barely made a mark on any map of Middlesex County. Back then in the 1940s, African Americans were all known as "coloreds." Many of this race and culture enjoyed different lifestyles. Some coloreds were barely scraping by to make it, while others had a modest lifestyle.

Those of the Caucasian or "white" ethnicity, on the other hand, appeared to have more of everything. They appeared to own all the properties on or near the water, all modes of transportation, as well as lovely homes, barns, etc. My family's home needed every repair imaginable. The house was so ragged that I had prayed it would burn down. But, being proud, I didn't want the community's sympathies, so I ended that wish.

My mother died when my three siblings and I were all very young. I was the oldest. We lived with my grandparents who tried their best to raise us, even though they had six grown children by this time. However, they never made us feel unwanted, just the opposite. Work in my hometown was seasonal. In the summer, my grandfather worked at the local sawmill or as a fisherman. In the winter, he worked as an oysterman or, weather permitting, at the local sawmill. Although my grandfather owned his own shabby boat, it was not of the quality that enabled him to make a living as a fisherman or oysterman; therefore, he worked for someone else.

My grandmother worked for little pay in the winter in the oyster canning factory. In the summer, she worked for low wages at the tomato canning factory or on large farms, picking beans, corn, tomatoes, or other summer vegetables. A big truck would come to our community around 7 a.m. and pick up my grandmother, the four of us and other community workers. We would ride to the farm, work all day for little or nothing and then return in the truck to our homes exhausted, dirty and hungry around 5 p.m.

Because we had no electricity, our work did not end at 5 p.m. My sisters and I, along with at least one older family member, would have to search in the nearby woods for trees to cut down and bring the wood to the yard where it was sawed into blocks, then chopped for the wood stove from which meals were prepared. During the winter, we had to again search, saw down and carry to the wood yard a different type of wood, one that was needed for stoves that heated the house. In addition to no electricity, we did not have running water, telephones, indoor bathrooms nor any form of transportation — no cars or trucks, not even a bicycle or wagon. Also, while there were no wells for drinking water, we walked to nearby neighbors for cooking and drinking water. Lugging those heavy pails from the neighbors meant that our containers were not very full when we finally reached home. We had a well in our yard, but it was only usable for washing clothes, bathing and scrubbing the floors. Sometimes during the summer months, the well would run dry, and we would have to wait until it replenished itself.

If we were blessed with a good rain, we could use the rainwater for different purposes. In the winter, the well would freeze over, and we would have to wait for it to thaw. Our school homework, when we finally got around to it, was often done by lamp light. Sometimes we were so tired from all the chores that by the time we got to homework, we were falling asleep. But, by the grace of God, we were pretty good students. No matter the situation, we were made to go to school every day.

The bus picked us up at the end of our road and off we went. We were sent to church every first and third Sunday of the month. Most of the time we had to walk the two miles to and from church. Our grandparents were God-fearing people. They established biblical principles in us and made certain we practiced what they taught. They had no problem "spoiling the child," yet, not "sparing the rod."

As I grew older, I realized my home was never a place that I wanted to invite anyone to for a sleepover. We had plenty of friends but not sleepover friends. Some of my school friends enjoyed sleepovers with their buddies, and sometimes even with their schoolteachers. It was a real treat and a big plus if you were invited overnight to a teacher's home. I spent one night with one of my teachers and her home was "oh so beautiful!" I did not know how to work the shower, so I did the usual wash up. I did not have a little girl's suitcase, so I brought my overnight wrinkled clothes in a bag (not sure what kind but probably a big brown paper bag). The teacher did not comment one way or the other. In my mind, she thought "poor baby." We didn't have much conversation while I was there, so I left feeling she really hadn't wanted me to come. I asked to spend the night with her, and she probably felt she couldn't say "no."

Now, when I reached the eighth grade, I invited my best girlfriend for a sleepover. I had already spent a night at her house, so it was only natural that I would reciprocate. I asked my grandparents if she could come for the night. They were fine with it, not understanding that I did not want to invite anyone to our house. I was poor, but proud! My grandmother was not a housekeeper; she was more accustomed to working on farms and at factories, and caring for chickens, ducks, pigs and, oh, the stray cats and dogs that showed up at our house. Over time, I learned some housekeeping techniques and became pretty good at making the house look habitable.

Well, my girlfriend came for the sleepover. I don't remember what we had for dinner, how we bathed for the night or how we got ready for school the next morning. We probably stayed up most of the night — lamps gone out — laughing and talking about nothing. All I know is that the event happened, and I was glad it was over.

It was not until February 2018, some 62 years later, that I attended a 75th surprise birthday party for my childhood girlfriend. At the party, I was given the opportunity to offer congratulatory remarks. Among other things, I mentioned the sleepover, saying something like: "As a young child, I envied you and your family because you all seemed to have been rich." After her birthday celebration, she telephoned me some days later to tell me what a pleasant surprise to see me — hadn't seen her in 10 years or so.

Her remarks to me were very special. She said, in her sweet, angelic voice, "I took exception to your remark that my family seemed rich." My friend explained, "When I came to spend the night with you, I thought you all were rich. I didn't see anything to complain about. In fact, I was glad I didn't have to share the bed with anyone except you. And your grandparents treated me with so much love and respect. I will never forget them."

My friend's father died in a boating incident, along with one of her aunts when she was just 10 years old. By the grace of God and family support, her mother raised seven very successful children. My mother died the same year from childbirth. By the grace of God and community support, our grandparents raised the four of us to be upstanding members of society. My revelation in all of this is that all I knew was that they lived in a better house, had running water, indoor bathrooms, electricity, telephones, etc., and that, in my eyesight, was rich.

My grandparents have passed away, and the old ragged house was bulldozed. However, before my grandmother died, after my grandfather passed, God blessed her to live in a new home with electricity, running water, indoor bathroom, telephone service and the like.

I can now say at this point that I guess "poor" is relative. Yes, the house was ragged and lacking but the good news is there was unspoken love. God was with us every step of the way and used our "lack of" so that we would appreciate the blessings he had in store. I can truly say God has and continues to bless us mightily. But God!

ENEMIES FACILITATED MY PROMOTION

By Tonya Barbee

I am a product of two hardworking parents. My late father, Woodrow W. Barbee, Jr., was an Army officer, Green Beret in the 82nd Airborne, Special Forces. My mother, Doris Barbee, now 80, was an administrator for college presidents at two East Coast Historically Black Colleges and Universities (HBCUs). My mother instilled in me a desire to be a school administrator and that is where I've been most of my 35-year career. I set forth to have great work ethics and to never settle. But what I have observed is that working hard is not always appreciated by others. However, I'm here to tell you, never stop doing your best in the workplace AND where you worship. You work for God after all, right?

Education is a must today. Many people are graduating from college with master's degrees, in addition to the basic four-year bachelor's degree, and can speak multiple foreign languages, as well. Besides my mother's example, God also used my experiences to stress the importance of education.

I left both Howard University in Washington, D.C. and North Carolina Central University in Durham, North Carolina within one or two semesters each, although the institutions had offered to pay my expenses — known as a"full ride." My excuse initially was that it was difficult for me to focus because I had married very young and had my handsome baby boy when I was 18. In addition, I felt like I was raising three kids: my new young husband, son, and myself. Every time I looked at my son, I knew I had to make the best of my life.

I took so many classes at Prince George's Community College (PGCC) that I eventually had enough credits to complete an associate degree. But I was not focused and didn't finish at PGCC, so I started taking classes at the University of Maryland, University College. Before long, I was divorced. Within five years, I was in love again and got married. This time, I had two beautiful girls who also were the apple of my eye.

My husband and I bought a beautiful new home in the Lake Arbor community of Mitchellville, Maryland. We had four bedrooms with a huge kitchen and deck to entertain our large families. It was a dream come true. Where I worked was great as well. I was an executive assistant for an educational institution affiliated with the U.S. Department of Agriculture. I had a wonderful relationship with my boss until I needed to stay with my dying father for 30 days in South Carolina.

Something changed when my boss saw a picture of my home on my desk. He had the audacity to say, "I didn't know your house looked THIS nice." I responded, "Sir, how did you expect my home to look?" Maybe I should have kept my mouth shut, because from that moment on he treated me differently. My performance reviews changed from "excellent" to "satisfactory."

When the boss said, "Tonya, I'm afraid we no longer have any more funding to send you to school," I was heartbroken. But worse, he became distant and sarcastic. However, every day I prayed for God to heal my heart: "Don't let me treat my boss like he is treating me." Then, I filed a complaint with the Equal Employment Opportunity Commission (EEOC) after noticing all the extra work I had done to ensure that our office remained afloat during my stay with my dad. Also, the funding for training that my boss denied me was still available to others. The mistreatment affected me so badly that I started getting migraines. My spirit was deflated.

Meanwhile, sadly, my second marriage ended in divorce too. But nine years later, I won my EEOC case, but the commissioner granted me "zero dollars" at the settlement hearing because I had moved on to another agency, received higher grades and basically "didn't look like what I said I went through." Technically, I didn't win because I got "zero" dollars. But, spiritually, I did win. I gained experience galore, got many free classes, and learned not to have personal pictures on my desk.

At my new agency, the Department of Defense, I thanked God every day for bringing me out and up! I had moved on to better pastures. I now had a boss who looked like me and treated employees fairly. I moved up three grades after he hired me! Praise God! Eventually, my boss moved on to another department, however. I was transferred to a new territory that moved me beyond what I could ever have imagined. I had completed my bachelor's degree at National-Louis University and worked on my MBA at that school a few years later. Finally, I achieved my educational goal! With faith and humility, I accomplished the mission.

My personal life was a roller coaster. Within the first few years at the new agency, I got married again and had a big, beautiful baby boy. I was in my early 40s with gigantic fibroids. The doctor said the baby would never make it to full term, but God blessed me. The doctor didn't factor God into the equation. Not only was there a baby in my uterus but he was a baby so big that for three weeks after delivery, I could not walk without severe pain. He had damaged my pelvic bone. I was sliding across the floor like Michael Jackson did with his famous moon walk. My feet couldn't leave the floor.

By the time I got back to work after maternity leave, I was given even more responsibilities. Before I could blink an eye, I had yet another boss and a different set of problems. Despite the turmoil and a rapidly developing hostile environment, my boss and coworkers didn't know I had a relationship with God. I prayed daily. And most importantly,

I prayed Psalm 37. I would recite the Scripture while walking in the office first thing each morning. Rumor has it, one of the employees from my team complained to officials that I was "ruining the atmosphere." I continued to pray and have faith that things would soon get better on the job. However, things grew worse and my migraines returned.

Then I had a severe fall that required surgery and caused me to miss six weeks of work. When I returned to work, there were no kind greetings or even one "welcome back" card. I learned two things: Don't expect people to treat you how you treat them and once someone shows you how they feel about you, why do you feel it's your responsibility to change their opinion of you? I knew then, it was time to leave and I started looking elsewhere for work.

I stepped up my faith. I remembered who my God was and the fact that He remembered me. I knew, He knew what was going on and would not let me down. He knew that I loved Him, and He would make it work for my good. I began to hold my head up high. I continued to do the best job that I could daily. I dressed well, my hair was always neatly coifed, and my makeup was flawless covering tear-stained cheeks. I wanted to look successful, although I didn't always feel successful.

Just when I thought I couldn't take it anymore, I was offered a very technical, detailed assignment in the Chief Operating Officer's directorate. See, things work out in God's timing, not our timing. I was clueless about the expectations of the assignment but accepted the detail. With God, all things are possible. My life changed immediately. It was like a new lease on my life. However, on the home front, I was divorced again. This time, the marriage was annulled because I married a bigamist. On the job, I registered for any class that would help me learn about internal controls and records management. There were nights when I would cry and ask God, "Why me?"

Why did God allow me to be set up like this? I also asked Him why it wasn't revealed to me about my child's father. I heard that still, small voice say that He did reveal things, but I didn't listen. Free will is no joke! One thing for sure, I learned I was hasty at making decisions in my personal life and that needed to change.

God gave me a big heart. What I had to learn was that I needed to slow down and put all my trust in God and not in man.

On the job, I performed the detail for one year and took all the required classes I needed for a better understanding of the tasks. When my job was announced to the general public, I was hired over at least 100 applicants. I had claimed *my* job, although my mentors told me I probably wouldn't get it. I not only had a leg up on the position, I had God in my life. And those who complained about me remain where they were. Now I understand Psalm 110:1, about making "your enemies a footstool for your feet." They often called on me to help them do THEIR jobs.

It's not always going to be rosy on the job. I worked 23 years in different positions. Through turmoil, keep your eyes on God and never trust in what man says he's going to do for you, whether you have no education or a doctorate. God is in control! When you keep Him in the forefront, no matter how difficult it may be, He will show you how He can use your enemies to facilitate your promotion. I thank God daily for what He has done in my life.

GOD WILL ALWAYS COME THROUGH

By Sidonie Becton, Esq.

"That is why, for Christ's sake, I delight in weaknesses, in insults, in hardships, in persecutions, in difficulties. For when I am weak, then I am strong." (2 Corinthians 12:10 NIV)

The Bible is filled with numerous references to the number "8" as being a symbol of resurrection and new beginnings. For me, 2018 was a journey of breaking, rebuilding, and establishing. Even in the toughest moments, God found a way to use my struggles to build my strength in Him and remind me of His promise for my life.

The year began with excitement. I was planning a wedding and studying for the Bar Exam! I shared the happy moments of deciding on a dress with my mom and finding a venue for what, I thought, would be an amazing winter wedding. Fast forward to a couple months later, I found myself in one of the most jarring situations I could imagine: Being told I wasn't enough for someone because of the color of my skin and my educational background. I was in disbelief. The years of praying together, supporting one another through some of our toughest times, and laying the foundation for what we thought would be a successful future all came to a sudden halt. To add insult to injury, a week after my engagement ended, I found out I did not pass the Bar Exam by five points.

I felt alone. No matter what anyone said, it didn't seem to help. For months, I cried to God, asking Him, "Why? Why me? How could You allow this?" As a black woman who was taught to follow her dreams, it was hard for me to understand how God could tell someone I'm not enough because of my skin color or academic achievements. I thought Proverbs 31 said that God looks at the heart and not the outward appearance? I was dumbfounded and confused.

At one of my lowest moments, I remembered something I was taught in church: No matter how you feel, still talk to God. Let Him know how you feel, even if you're upset with Him. From then on, I began talking to God, not just in my morning and evening prayers, but throughout the day. As I drew closer to God, I could feel my relationship growing stronger with Him. Having a different relationship with Him, I asked God to, again, show me the purpose in ending that relationship. When I didn't hear from Him for a couple of days, I became upset.

In the middle of the night, I cried out for God to just let me know that He heard me! The following day, an older gentleman at my job, whom I previously only exchanged pleasantries with and who did not know my situation, pulled me aside and said, "God hears you. He knows who you are. He is protecting you." I almost cried right then and there. In my time with God that night, I realized there is more to being equally yoked with someone than just claiming you're a Christian outwardly; you must be equally yoked in the spirit and understanding of Christ, as well.

While all this was going on, I decided to study for the Bar Exam again. I tried my best to remain positive throughout the process, but it was hard to focus. One thing I knew for sure was that God wanted me to rely on Him and only Him during this time. So, even when I couldn't focus to study, I prayed for guidance and discernment. This isn't something I'd done before. But I decided to just trust Him and the plans He had for me. After I came to peace with everything, it was amazing how things began moving in my life. God began placing people in my life who would support and check on me, even when I didn't know I needed it! I became more active in ministries at church, connecting with people who have become friends and mentors.

I received notifications on the same day of two job interviews, one from an organization I'd dreamed of working for. Within days of one of the interviews, I was given a job offer. My worry and stress about employment were over! In November 2018, I learned I passed the Bar Exam! The results came just in time for my dad's birthday and was the best gift I could give my family for the holiday season!

I struggled with writing this testimony because I never saw myself going through this situation. I recently attended a church service in New York where the pastor addressed distractions and not allowing them to keep you from seeing the work God is doing to move you to the next level. During that service, I received a confirmation email certifying my swearing into the Washington, D.C. Bar. It was in that moment that I knew I had to share my story with you.

You have a specific purpose in your life. Even when the outcome isn't what you hoped for, God can use your lowest moments for His victory! His fulfillment of the promises He's made to us do not always look the way we thought they would. But this doesn't mean He's forgotten you. Moving forward with wisdom, resilience, and a stronger faith, I know that no matter what lies around the corner, God will ALWAYS come through!

UNSCRIPTED INTERRUPTION

By Rev. Yasmine Bell-Flemons

Women of every shade, size, and age have been dealing with life's interruptions since the beginning of time — the loss of a child, divorce, heart disease, cancer or neurological disorders. Our mothers, sisters, aunties and good girlfriends have not allowed these disruptions to completely overtake their body, mind, or soul. For what has not killed us, has only made our faith stronger in God. Even when the battles become difficult, women have stood strong and courageous in the face of death, knowing nothing is impossible for God. While we all have testimonies, this is my story, how I fought my battle with multiple sclerosis by embracing the unexpected.

This unexpected interruption of my life began in the fall of 1993. I was about to embark on a major collaboration with a household-name company to develop a reading program for inner city girls who need after-school tutoring. I removed nonessential appointments from my schedule and contacted the company's corporate office to begin setting timelines for a draft proposal. As time moved swiftly, I began having some problems with keeping my balance. Each morning, I would fall getting out of bed. It was difficult for me to walk up or down stairwells. I was not able to grasp items because I couldn't make a fist to brace myself or cushion my fall. I could not lift my legs to climb onto ladders. I began to use home delivery services because holding grocery bags and getting the items home and in the pantry were nearly impossible. Headaches and body pain were regular. No matter how I attempted to rest my body, the pain never seemed to dissipate.

When I realized my mobility was failing and that the dizziness, headaches and body pain were increasing, I urgently sought the help of a neurologist. I was forced to place all events, plans and collaborations on hold as I sought medical attention. I finally decided to contact my primary care doctor. After several medical appointments ranging from pain management doctors to neurological specialists, I was given a temporary diagnosis of benign positional vertigo (BPV).

After the BPV diagnosis, my bodily pain worsened. I was in a state of confusion, not fully understanding what to do or which way to turn. One day while having lunch at The Dabney in Northwest Washington, D.C., a friend recommended a specialist in neurological disorders. With the initial appointment, the doctor ordered a series of blood tests, X-rays, body scans and an MRI. Two weeks later, the doctor called to say, "you have multiple sclerosis," which is a degenerative neurological disorder that eats away at the myelin tissue that surrounds the central nervous system of the body. I knew with that phone call that day my life would be forever changed.

Certainly, this was not written in the script of the life I had imagined for myself. I had plans on the table, major business plans to discuss future educational business collaborations with some major community stakeholders. *Multiple who?* was my response as I questioned this unanticipated ailment. I was due to start a post-graduate program in educational psychology in the next two months. I questioned the reasoning again in my mind. *Sclerosis what, how do you spell that S-c-e-l-r?* Not now life, not now!! I have way too much on my plate for all these unexpected interruptions. *Degenerative disorder that affects where?*

I've been in church since I can remember. Baptized at the age of 8, I worked as a junior missionary who visited the sick and shut-ins and sang in the choir. Heck, I even joined the Girl Scouts at age 9. Church was all I knew, so praying to the Lord was a familiar space for me. However, this would be the first time in my life that my faith was tested.

I began to call on the Lord: "God, can you please stretch Your mighty hand over this mishap situation and stop all these unexpected, unscripted interruptions?" God responded by bringing to my remembrance the Apostle Paul, who was a faithful follower of Jesus Christ also. Paul prayed to be released from his weakness, however, he received this answer: *"My grace is sufficient for you, for My strength is made perfect in weakness."* (2 Corinthians 12:7-10 NKJV)

It is in these unscripted, interrupted painful periods of life that we, as women, can rest peacefully knowing that God will and does show up anytime, anyplace — unexpectedly to bless his daughters. God is predictable in His unpredictability. The unexpected things in life never catch Him by surprise or off guard. To every "she-ro" who wrestles with telling her story, please understand and believe that God delights in surprising us, in revealing the ways He is not like us, and showing us His power when we least expect His blessings, which are *"exceedingly, abundantly, above what you could ever ask, think, or believe."* (Ephesians 4:20 NKJV)

Yes, I've had to make some daily living adjustments to accommodate my unexpected health challenges. I use my cane when walking and standing become difficult. I am not ashamed to ask for help when I'm out in public. And, when I am tired, I rest. Currently, I live a fully functioning life. I travel. I teach around the East Coast. I conduct workshops across the country on leadership and readiness/preparedness for the Joint Services, which include the Army, Navy, Air Force, and the Marine Corps.

I enjoy volunteering in my local community in Charles County, offering free workspace as a safe-haven for women and young girls interested in life-skills seminars. I am on staff as an associate minister at First Baptist Church of Highland Park, where I enjoy serving my pastor and fellow comrades in the gospel.

One day I want to hear my Savior say, *"Here's the woman who never gave up. Despite her obstacles, she kept pushing through. This woman gave her all in the community to serve those less fortunate. She combated an unexpected neurological disorder and stuck to the script. Yasmine Bell-Flemons, come on up, well done thou good and faithful servant."*

ETERNALLY GRATEFUL

By Catherine T. Bennett

One weekday morning in the early 1980s, the sun was shining ever so brightly. It was a beautiful morning! My husband worked the early shift that week, so I was left to get our two children, ages 6 and 13, prepared for school.

When I entered their bedrooms, they appeared to be sleeping comfortably. After waking them, they started their morning routines of brushing their teeth, washing their face and hands, putting on school uniforms, and eating breakfast. I kept a checklist to ensure my children took to school everything they needed for the day — backpacks filled with completed homework, school supplies and lunch boxes crammed with a sandwich, juice, and a snack.

We left the house and piled into my car. I checked my mirrors, placed the gear in drive and pulled away from the curb. At a nearby intersection, a driver struck my car and the impact pushed it across the street towards oncoming traffic. My children and I were terrified. My car was demolished. But my children were my main concern. They were crying. We all had shattered glass in our hair but, from what I could tell, there were no broken bones. An ambulance rushed all three of us to the hospital, where my husband was waiting. We were treated and released.

When I reflect upon this accident, I thank God that my children were not injured. I now realize that God had placed a hedge around us for protection. Although there were no serious injuries, I suffered whiplash for a few days, wore a neck brace, and attended several therapy sessions.

I sometimes wondered "how did we survive?" But now I realize, it was by the goodness and grace of God that we escaped with only minor bumps, bruises and cuts. God kept me because He apparently was not finished with me at that time in my life.

I was baptized into the Catholic faith as a child, but in October 2011, God allowed me to be born again and baptized at First Baptist Church of Highland Park. Glory to His name!

I now know why Psalm 91 is one of my favorite Scriptures – it is a prayer of protection. This Psalm shows God's different levels of protection and how each is filled with the goodness and power of God. Because I love the Lord, He promises to rescue me, and because I acknowledge His name, He promises to protect me (v.14). I unquestionably was protected the morning of this accident. The Lord faithfully works on behalf of those who love Him. Each night before going to bed, I feel delivered when I read Psalm 91.

Just as I learned after the accident where God protected the three of us, I now know, without a doubt, that He continues to do so in our lives!

THROUGH THE RAIN AND THROUGH THE STORMS

By Janice L. Boone

One morning while on my way to work in the early 1960s, I was involved in an automobile accident on 8th Street in Northwest Washington, D.C. A woman driving a Volkswagen ran through a red traffic light and crashed into a car driven by my fiancé. The woman's 2-year-old son was thrown from the car and died instantly. I smashed into the front window and was rushed to Providence Hospital, where I spent several weeks in the Intensive Care Unit in serious condition with severe head and facial wounds.

The woman and her husband came to visit me in the hospital that evening in the midst of their sadness and sorrow over the death of their son. She told me that at the time of the accident she had just dropped her husband off at work and was traveling back home to continue packing because the family was preparing to move. The boy was standing in the front seat of the car; there were no seatbelt requirements during that time. The wife was emotionally upset, crying throughout their time with me. While I appreciated their visit, I realized that God had spared my life. A few weeks later, I was discharged from the hospital and returned home to my 5-year-old son and two daughters, who were ages 7 and 9 at the time.

Many years later, I became sick with a very high fever. The medical staff and attending physicians were unable to identify the cause of my high fever. After many tests and treatments, I was admitted and hospitalized. Finally, doctors discovered I had something called sarcoidosis, an immune system disorder. My friends often reminded me that this was the same disease that eventually killed Bernie Mac, the stage name for the African American stand-up comedian and actor Bernard Jeffrey McCullough. Nevertheless, once again God was with me, and I was certain I would be all right during my illness.

During my illness, I found joy in reading God's Word. I was convinced that God was watching over me. I didn't always understand the full interpretation and meaning of the Bible passages right away, but I would feel such peace, joy, and comfort after reading and studying. A few weeks later, I was discharged from the hospital. While recuperating, I would read the Bible during visits to doctor's offices or to fill my time elsewhere. I would not go anywhere without my Bible during this time. A few months later, my medicines were reduced, and eventually discontinued. I was doing well! That was many years ago. Even to this blessed day, there is no sign of sarcoidosis or high fever.

Shortly thereafter, in 1992, I found myself walking down the aisle of First Baptist Church of Highland Park in Landover, Maryland. I joined the church and gave my heart to the Lord. As God would have it, I met a quiet and gentle lady who agreed to disciple me. The first thing she shared was the power of Psalm 91. I learned that chapter from verse one to 16. Each day I would write the verses out on a note pad, jotting the day's date in the margin. To this day, I can recite verbatim those verses that make up Psalm 91. I've learned a lot, especially that God loves me, even though I am having a rough time. Nobody but God will reach down and pick you up, heal your diseased body, calm your troubled mind, and let you know without a doubt that you will never walk alone!

JUST TRUST HIM. HOW WONDERFUL GOD IS!!! AMEN!!!

A NEW WOMAN IN CHRIST

By Joann Antoinette Borges-Palmer

I was baptized, as an infant, at St. Martins Catholic Church in Washington, D.C. in 1956 with two Godparents, Ruby Young and Joseph Monteiro, who were friends of my parents. I made my First Holy Communion and Confirmation, which were the requirements of the Catholic Church and its faith. I went to confession and received communion regularly. I attended Sunday School every week, learned all the prayers, and recited the entire Catholic Mass by heart. My mother was left to raise 13 children after my father vanished from our lives. Undaunted, my mother took us to church every Sunday. But what I saw the rest of the week did not reflect anything I heard in Sunday School or at church.

I know I prayed a lot, but I did not quite understand why all the older people around me were teaching me, advising me, introducing me to things of the world, such as sex, drugs, alcohol, cigarettes and marijuana. I stopped attending the Catholic Church, moved to the Methodist AME Zion

Church, changed to an Episcopal church, then Holiness, and finally to a Baptist church. I never understood the different denominations and what they meant. All I knew was that I had faith in something bigger than me and talked to God through Jesus Christ after I was told I could go to God for myself and did not have to go to a priest or anyone else. I was told I had to have my own relationship with God and could not get to heaven on the "family plan."

During my teenage years, I was exposed to the life of entertainment. My sisters were go-go dancers and passed that legacy down to me. They introduced me to their connections and managers, and I picked up where they left off. I danced with The Dells, The Manhattans, Kool and the Gang, The ChiLites, Chuck Brown and the Soul Searchers, Rare Essence, Trouble Funk, Black Ivory, and Bobby Womack, just to name a few. I performed at Wilmer's Park as The Parkettes during my summer vacation.

Imagine when I returned to school in the fall and was asked to write an essay on what I did during my summer vacation. I had to make up something that sounded like the summer vacation of a seventh, eighth or ninth grader. It was nothing for Chaka Khan or Walter Jackson's limousines to pull up in front of our door. The neighbors would watch to see who was going in the Borges' house this time. We performed at cabarets, The Mark IV, The Warner Theater, Panorama Room, and several clubs in the Washington D.C. metropolitan area, known as the DMV.

It's a good thing no one ever asked for identification back then because all those establishments would have lost their licenses.

When my mother died and I did not feel like I belonged anywhere or to anyone, I married a man who had a great family that ate dinner together, went on vacations together, and looked out for each other. Being a part of that family made me feel like I was loved, even if they were pretending only because they loved the man I married, not necessarily me. My husband was 6 years older than me. I started dating him when I was 13 years old and in junior high school. He worked after high school graduation and took some college classes. However, he became abusive, beating me if men made passes at me or when I found him cheating with other women.

Drugs began to consume his life and he would send me to men who sold drugs, knowing what they required from me for payment. My husband was my husband, my three sons' daddy, and my pimp. I did not love myself enough to leave and desperately wanted my sons to have a father, unlike me who never knew or saw my father. I thought a bad father was better than no father. I stayed in that relationship for more than 20 years. I left him and my children to stay in a safe house until I could get clean off the drugs, divorce him and get custody of my children.

I accepted Jesus Christ as my Lord and Savior while I was still in my addiction and asked HIM to help me because I could not do it on my own; and, that was more than 40 years ago. I went back to drugs several times after that and thought I wasn't worthy of God's love, so I stayed away from family and friends. I would get clean for 5 years then go back to drugs; get clean, then go back over and over until I completely surrendered about 20 years ago and HE took the desire from me. Praise God!

I met my second husband at an Alcoholics Anonymous meeting. I continued to attend these meetings periodically, to share my story of hope and encouragement to people like me and those still struggling with addictions. After a year of marriage, I was called at work to come home only to find that my husband had committed suicide by hanging himself in our home. People asked me, how did I stay in that house after that and I told them I was not afraid of the dead.

Husband number three was someone I met some 34 years ago, and he swore he was going to marry me one day. I took his money and his drugs and said, "okay if you think so." He married someone else because I kept saying "no." That woman eventually died in his home from a drug overdose. I kept encouraging him to get some help for his grieving and his drug addiction, but eventually I stopped going around that negative environment. I did not want to be pulled back into that life.

Several years later, after losing my second husband, he called me to offer his condolences and we started communicating on a regular basis. He seemed to have taken my advice and changed his life. We dated, joined First Baptist Church of Highland Park and were baptized. We later got married. It was great the first year, then he changed, falling into mental health episodes. One morning he was not up at his usual time. When I opened his door to check on him, he was lying in the bed. His chest was not going up and down like normal. I screamed because I knew he was dead, the second husband to die in my home. It was time to go.

I had a lot of bad things happen to me, but I realize now that they happened to me because, even though I did not know my earthy father, I've always trusted my Heavenly Father. He walks with me and He talks with me and carried me most of my life. And now, He told me to go tell everyone my story and how good God is. For there is no respecter of persons with God. If He did it for me, He can do it for you.

I'm like the willow tree; I may bend but I do not break. As the wind blows, as storms rage on in the world, the willow tree will bend and will remain strong. Rarely, can the fierce storm cause it to break. You see, there is a secret that the willow tree has learned over the centuries. The secret lies in its roots. As bendable as the willow tree may appear to be, deep beneath Earth the roots of the tree are strong, solid and secure. I know that I'm rooted in the Word of God and without Him I'm nothing.

God is my compass, my driving force, my healer, my teacher, my intercessor, and the center of my joy. So, in the words of gospel music artist and Pastor Marvin Sapp, *"so if you see me cry, It's just a sign that I'm, I'm still alive. I got some scars, but I'm still alive. Despite calamity, He still has a plan for me. And it's working for my good. And it's building my testimony."*

Each day is a new beginning for me and each day something else drops off. I pray daily. I exercise daily. I eat healthier, and I thank God daily that I am not that person I use to be — but a new creature in Christ.

THERE'S NO PLACE LIKE HOME

By Joyce Brooks

I am a native "Washtonian" — WASH-TOE-NEE-AN, just like my mother and her mother. I, 1. Didn't move here right after I was born; 2. Was not born here and raised somewhere else; and, 3. Haven't been here for so long that I might as **WELL** be a "Washtonian." **I AM ONE!** I praise God for having a "native son" and four beautiful "native grandchildren."

My roots go back to 1896 in Southwest Washington, D.C., where my maternal grandmother was born after her family moved from Caroline County, Virginia. Grandma and Pop were among the first African American families to purchase a home in a new development in Northeast Washington called Kingman Park, located off Benning Road. This home is still occupied almost 90 years later by me and my son and will always be considered *the house* by family members and friends.

I remember stories that my grandmother shared with me about buying her new home in 1929 for $3,600, an amount that was considered enormous at that time. Grandma told me how she and Pop saved for their down payment and how blessed they felt to be able to buy a house to raise their two sons and my mom, who was 6 months old when they moved in. They chose a house near the farthest end of the street, away from the anticipated heavy Benning Road traffic. How right they were! There once was an underground tunnel that stretched from one side of Benning Road to the other to avoid the heavy traffic, but that was removed many years ago.

Our neighbors were more than just the people next door or the folks up the street. They were our extended family, and everybody knew each other and got along with one another. Each family took pride in their property and worked hard to keep up the appearance of their homes and yards. A portion of the Robert F. Kennedy Stadium parking lot is now situated where there once was a dormitory for young ladies who had come to the nation's capital to work for the federal government. My grandparents and I would sit on the porch and offer conversation and lemonade to all who passed our home. Many of these ladies became lifelong family friends and one, from Little Rock, Arkansas, married my uncle and continued to live in the District of Columbia until her recent passing at the young age of 99 years.

My friends and I spent many a Saturday afternoon in the Langston Theater, catching the latest movies and then on to the Miles Long Sandwich Shop, Wiggins Carryout, or Sporty's

Carryout for a meal afterwards. The A&P, Dickmann's Market, and Gordons were the neighborhood grocery stores. When I ventured out of Kingman Park with my cousins or neighborhood friends in tow, we would put our quarter into the city transit bus and ride down to H Street Northeast to shop at H.L. Greens, Kopy Kat, McBride's, or John's Bargains. Many of my friends couldn't wait to move out of the neighborhood, but I was never in a rush to go. I always thought of the neighborhood as a great place to live and I loved my home! My grandparents taught me at an early age that we should take care of what we have and that being neighborly was natural. Grandma and Pop's motto was always "All Come — Welcome," and I still live by that creed to this day!

God has blessed me to live in this home for more than 50 years, enabling me to carry out my grandparents' dream of homeownership and passing on the tradition to my son and grandchildren. I can't imagine living anywhere other than in Kingman Park. The same loving home that my grandparents lived in and raised their children is where I was raised and where my grandchildren also call "home."

I enjoy travelling from city to city, country to country, and often people ask, "You aren't from here are you?" My answer is always a resounding, "No, I'm a third-generation 'Washtonian' from Kingman Park and proud of it!"

GOD IS NOT SANTA CLAUS

By Ironia M. Broyles

My first name is Ironia, which I learned is a feminine Latin word that in English means "irony." One of the dictionary's meaning of irony is "deliberately and especially the opposite of the literal meaning, and contrary to what one expects, and is often amusing as a result."

As a child, I equated God to Santa Claus, who I thought would reward me at Christmas time if I had been "good" all year or would not reward me if I had been 'naughty." That was what I was taught. So, each Christmas, I made an extra effort to be good. I shared my toys more and tried not to lose my temper, etc.

One Christmas Eve, as I fondly and vividly remember, although at this age my memories are rather vague, I would be too afraid to go to the bathroom at night because I thought that Santa Claus would not leave my toys if I was awake. Even without the thought of Christmas, I always sought to be good as a child, even if it was at the expense of my five brothers and sisters. For example, I would tattle on them to my parents and try to correct them when I thought they were out of line. In fact, while growing up, I tried to meet what I thought were everyone's expectations of me, working to do well in my own strength.

When I was around 13 years old, my Sunday School teacher at Third Baptist Church in Washington, D.C., Mrs. Alice Hawkins, led me to the Lord, explaining the fundamentals of allowing the Lord to be my Savior. She used: *"For God so loved the world, that He gave His only begotten Son, that whosoever believeth in Him should not perish, but have everlasting life."* (John 3:16 KJV)

I remember going on my first trip to New York City with my Sunday School class. Mrs. Hawkins had paid for my ticket because my mother could not afford the trip. The girls in the class and I shared a room and I remember waking up one night and hearing some of the girls laughing at me because they thought I was *too* good. At that time I was not dating or wearing makeup and was very quiet.

By the time I reached adulthood, however, I had grown tired of trying to meet everyone's expectations. I rebelled, going the way of the world. After some heartbreaks, and ungodly situations and relationships, the Lord led me into a closer relationship with Himself. Today, I realize that my past situation helps me to identify with the women we minister to in the Upper Marlboro, Maryland Correctional facility. I am the coordinator of that ministry.

On December 18, 1983, I rededicated my life to the Lord, after listening to a very convicting sermon by Rev. Stacy Middleton, who at that time was an associate minister at First Baptist Church of Highland Park in Landover, Maryland. On January 8, 1984, I was baptized again, and the Holy Spirit gave me a confirmation of joy that I, to this day, cannot explain.

Some of the Bible verses, all King James version, that helped me through my journey and continue to minister to me today are: John 3:16; 2 Corinthians 9:15; John 8:36; 1 John 5:11-12; and 2 Corinthians 5.

Second Corinthians 9:15, says, *"Thanks be unto God for His unspeakable gift."* My gift of eternal life cannot be adequately explained. But, I know that I could not nor did anything, to gain the gift of eternal life, which is salvation. All I had to do was to trust in Jesus Christ as my Lord and Savior. What irony this is! All those years of trying to please God in my own strength, yes, and even after salvation! But then John 8:36 (KJV) says, *"If the Son therefore shall make you free, ye shall be free indeed."*

I am free in the Lord, not bound by my own perception of myself or even of another's. Hallelujah! Finally, 1 John 5:11-12 (KJV) says, *"And this is the record, that God hath given to us eternal life, and this life is in His Son. He that hath the Son hath life; and he that hath not the Son of God hath not life."*

God is not Santa Claus, zapping me if I am naughty! I don't have to be afraid of Him. I remember the time that I was too afraid to get out of bed because I thought that Santa Claus would not leave me any toys! How funny is that? What irony! I am firmly gripped in the Hand of my Savior! I am firmly held and protected in this world! And when I die, Scripture states that absent from the body, present with the Lord, which is taken from 2 Corinthians 5:8.

While my earthly name of Ironia means 'irony,' I have a new name that is already written in Glory and it is mine — all mine! *"He that hath an ear, let him hear what the Spirit saith unto the churches; To him that overcometh will I give to eat of the hidden manna, and will give him a white stone, and in the stone a new name written, which no man knoweth saving he that receiveth it."* (Revelation 2:17 KJV)

Some may say that living on this earth beats the alternative of death, but guess what? My body may be in the grave, but my soul will be forever with the Lord! If you have accepted Jesus Christ as your Lord and Savior, living on this earth does not beat the alternative; but if you have not accepted God's plan of salvation, yes, living on this earth does beat the alternative because you are designated to spend eternity in hell when you die. What irony — the world's view of death is so contrary to God's way!

SEEING BEYOND PAIN, INJURY, AND STRESS

By Wanda Cartwright

I love to read stories about people who overcome seemingly insurmountable challenges to accomplish wonderful works. One of my favorite stories comes from the book of Ruth. It is a story that speaks volumes about overcoming obstacles. During a challenging time in my life, it spoke to me of how God sustains us amid debilitating crisis. It also taught me about how, even while we suffer, God positions us to bless others.

Two years after I lost my mother to diabetes in 2002, I became ill with blocked intestines, a nearly fatal condition that I suspected developed from working excessively day and night on a job with many projects but few staff members. I was hospitalized for nearly a month. When I was released from the hospital, I spent almost three months recovering at home. I feebly prayed for God's strength. Eventually, I regained enough strength to return to work, but I lacked the stamina that I had before my illness. I began worrying about how long I would be able to survive on this job in my diminished condition.

A few years after my illness, I attended a women's conference. One of the guest speakers gave a presentation about Naomi, the mother-in-law of Ruth, a Moabite woman whose name is a moniker for one of the books in the Old Testament of the Bible. I listened to the speaker as she unfolded a story about a woman whom I'd practically ignored when I'd read the four-chapter book in the past. The highlights:

- Naomi, her husband, Elimelech, and their two sons, Mahlon and Chilion left Bethlehem to escape famine and settled in the country of Moab.

- Sometime after settling in Moab, Naomi's husband, Elimelech dies.

- Naomi and her sons continue living in Moab. Her sons both marry Moabite women, one named Orpah and the other named Ruth.

- Naomi, her sons and their wives continue to live in Moab until both sons die without producing heirs.

- Naomi learns that there is no longer famine in her home of Bethlehem. She decides to return home and advises her daughters-in-law to return to their parents in Moab.

- Ruth and Orpah weep at the prospect of separating from Naomi. Orpah, however, does as she is advised and stays in Moab. Ruth insists on traveling with Naomi to Bethlehem.

- Naomi and Ruth are cordially received back in Bethlehem, but Naomi is bitter and depleted from all the tragedy in her life.

- In the meantime, Ruth seeks employment in one of the local fields and chances upon land owned by one named Boaz, a wealthy man who happens to be a relative of Elimelech.

- Ruth informs Naomi about working in Boaz's field.

- When Naomi learns about Boaz, she coaches Ruth about how to win his favor.

- Ruth follows Naomi's instructions.

- Eventually Ruth and Boaz wed and created a son.

- Naomi nursed the son, and they all became a part of the ancestral line of King David.

Hearing the story of Naomi was a divine gift. There in the pages of the Bible was a woman who suffered to the point of personal depletion. Yet, despite all she had lost, she was loved and revered by two daughters-in-law, loved by family and friends from her home town and had wealthy connections. She doubted that she had anything left in her life to offer. Yet, she mentored her daughter-in-law Ruth who ultimately blessed her and helped to usher her into a season of triumph.

Naomi's story helped me to see beyond pain from losing a loved one, injury from illness or stress from excessive work-place demands. It directed my focus to the family, friends and resources that God had placed in my life. It taught me to be ever-mindful of how well we float even when it feels like we're sinking.

Naomi's story also helped me to find ways to bless others while navigating life's storms. Recently, I decided to engage in a buddy system project with a co-worker. We've agreed to share ideas to help each other to tackle challenges that we may experience on the job. I see an opportunity to share the story of Naomi in our not so distant future.

THE LORD WILL MAKE A WAY SOMEHOW

By Wendy A. Cartwright

"And my God shall supply all your need according to His riches in glory by Christ Jesus." (Philippians 4:19 NKJV)

There are many promises in the Holy Bible, and each one deserves its own story. However, if I had to pick one to which I must bear witness, it is the promise mentioned in Philippians 4:19.

As a child, my parents taught my sister, brother and me to pray and to be thankful for everything around us: my mother and father, our home, family, friends, school, the food we ate, the toys we had, etc. But growing up, I really couldn't appreciate the sacrifices made to obtain the "everyday necessities" that many people in the world go without.

Through college and law school, and finding employment in the legal profession, I first began to see how God kept me safe and secure, and placed persons in my path who provided for my needs. When I became an attorney in a private law practice with one colleague, I truly began to understand that when I maintained my daily devotional relationship with God, I could see Him providing for all my needs just as He promised.

As the owner of a small law practice for more than 28 years, the reality is that, despite the many hours of hard work, there are times when the bills pile up and the money is low. That doesn't even include your own personal bills. Then, during those times, unanticipated costs rise as well, such as sudden car repairs, or a child in college needs money, etc. Every time periods of need in my life have arisen, God has met that need true to His Word.

I do not write this essay to *explain* these events that I have experienced, because I do not know "how" God provided for my needs and the needs of those around me. I just know that He did, and I am here to bear witness. I can only tell you that when I needed encouragement, God sent a friend that encouraged me, or a sermon that ministered directly to my needs, usually through Pastor Henry P. Davis, III, at First Baptist Church of Highland Park in Landover, Maryland. When I was injured, God healed me through caring health professionals, and some of my church family encouraged me along the way!

When I needed to make a decision, after prayer and meditation, God sent me "wise counsel" that gave me the advice I needed or affirmed the decision(s) I made. When money was needed, my financial needs were met also.

"I have been young, and now am old; yet I have not seen the righteous forsaken, nor his descendants begging bread." (Psalm 37:25 NKJV) I believe this verse, which preceded Paul's letter in Philippians, promises us that when we believe that God will do as He promised, and strive to be righteous according to His Word, God will provide not only for our needs, but also for the needs of our children, and our children's children. Over the years, I have seen God move in the lives of families, clients, and persons who have endured tragedy, trials and tribulations, and I watched as God provided for their needs.

If you are asking yourself, "how do I become righteous, so I can receive God's promises?" Start at the beginning as I did. First, I believe God is the Father, Son and Holy Spirit. I believe God is everything that He says He is, and that His Holy Word is true, so I work daily to strengthen my relationship with Him.

Second, I believe that prayer changes things. I have seen honest, open prayer change events, heal lives, deliver persons in bondage, and impact persons who have no concept of prayer. When you talk to God every day, you will learn why obedience is better than sacrifice, why tithing is not optional, that God orders our steps. That the urgent matters in our lives should not take the place of the important ones, and that God loved us so much that He sent His Son Jesus as a sacrifice to die in our place for our sins so that we can have eternal life. When you are in need, talk to God; ask Him specifically to meet your need, and He will provide.

Third, I choose to live a righteous life, and to be like Christ. Psalm 34:19 says *"the righteous person faces many troubles, but the Lord comes to the rescue each time."* I have been involved in many legal battles in which my prayers were answered, and Jesus intervened in the situation. When you have a relationship with Christ, you learn not to worry about anything, but to pray about everything. You also learn that unless you are prompted by the Holy Spirit, never hurry to make decisions, to take action or respond to someone just to get it done. The Holy Spirit will guide you and tell you what you should do.

While striving to be like Christ, I pray daily for wisdom. James 1:5 says *"If you need wisdom, ask our generous God and he will give it to you."* God's wisdom will save you from evil people (Proverbs 2:12), and Proverbs 4:7 states that we should *"get wisdom and develop good judgment."* In today's society, we need all the wisdom we can get.

As my journey to be a servant of Christ continues, I don't know what my future holds, but I know who holds my future. I know that through every stage of my journey, God will continue to be present with me and provide for my every need. If you truly believe, He will do the same for you, too.

HOW TO SURVIVE WHEN SURROUNDED BY LITTLE OR NO FAITH:

God Has All Power, Authority And Is A Healer

By Robin Cashwell

On Sunday, June 8, 2013, I went to the emergency room at Georgetown University Hospital in Washington, D.C. because I was very tired. I had been so exhausted I could not carry my pocketbook or walk to my car after waking up in the morning and getting ready for work. I had never experienced this type of fatigue before. I also was constantly eating jumbo cups of ice throughout the day. I had an appetite and slept well, but still woke up exhausted each day.

I had no energy to do small tasks such as cooking, washing dishes, showering and bathing. When I arrived at the hospital, the doctors wanted to admit me for a blood transfusion.

I refused the offer and asked them to come up with another plan. I decided to leave the hospital and asked to be discharged. I did not want or need anybody else's blood in my body. I've always made daily declarations over my health, proclaiming that "Jesus has already done everything for me and has already given me everything I need in my body!"

Some of the doctors told me to stop speaking about my spiritual beliefs and focus on reality. I immediately shared my faith with all the doctors because they were standing around my bed in the emergency room trying to figure out how to help me. "We've never had a case like this before," one of the doctors said. My iron levels were at 4 mg, compared with the 11 to 15 mg that were normal for women at that age. Doctors said I should have died or would not live to see Monday, which was the next day. The lab work did not lie. Yet, I still refused the blood transfusion. I shared my faith, cited Scriptures and just believed God at His Word. I knew I already had everything I needed: my faith and a peace.

These are the Bible verses I meditated on:

- *"And this same God who takes care of me will supply all your needs from his glorious riches, which have been given to us in Christ Jesus."* (Philippians 4:19)

- *"Don't worry about anything; instead, pray about everything. Tell God what you need, and thank him for all he has done. Then you will experience God's peace, which exceeds anything we can understand. His peace will guard your hearts and minds as you live in Christ Jesus. And now, dear brothers and sisters, one final thing. Fix your thoughts on what is true, and honorable, and right, and pure, and lovely, and admirable. Think about things that are excellent and worthy of praise. Keep putting into practice all you learned and received from me — everything you heard from me and saw me doing. Then the God of peace will be with you."* (Philippians 4:6-9)

- *"And we know that God causes everything to work together for the good of those who love God and are called according to His purpose for them."* (Romans 8:28)

- *"... Truly I tell you, if you have faith as small as a mustard seed, you can say to this mountain, 'Move from here to there,' and it will move. Nothing will be impossible for you."* (Matthew 17:20 NIV)

These Scriptures gave me the strength to believe *all* things are possible, even if it contradicts the world's way of thinking and believing. We are to have higher expectations in Jesus Christ!!

I learned in Luke 13:19, that our faith starts off small and has the potential to grow, expand and blossom beyond our normal intelligence, and capacity to visualize miraculous signs, and wonders. The New Living Translation states that our faith *"is like a tiny mustard seed that a man planted in a garden; it grows and becomes a tree, and the birds make nests in its branches."* (Luke 13:19)

The apostles said to the Lord in Luke 17:5-6 NIV, *"Increase our faith!"* He replied, *"If you have faith as small as a mustard seed, you can say to this mulberry tree, 'Be uprooted and planted in the sea,' and it will obey you."*

I never got the blood transfusion. My diagnosis was fibroids. I could not undergo embolism surgery to have the fibroids removed because my asthma reduced to 50/50 my chances of waking up from surgery. I prayed and felt that the Lord did not want me to undergo surgery. Surgery is not for everybody!! I have learned just because the doctor says you need surgery, does not mean God wants you to have surgery. The Bible says, *"Be anxious for nothing, but in everything by prayer and supplication with thanksgiving let your requests be made known to God."* (Philippians 4:6 NKJV)

A treatment plan was designed to sustain me and help me survive. The main doctor's treatment plan for me came after I asked the unbelieving doctors to leave the room. They left my bedside, rebuking me for proclaiming and speaking my faith. I did not need their help because I knew we would never agree. They did not know MY God!! And, their opposition was not as strong as my relationship with God and His Son, Jesus.

Today, 5 years later, I am still on the treatment plan. I am living a blessed life!! I did not die, and I am going to be taken off the medicine soon. God has healed me, and its manifestation has been revealed. The fibroids finally shrunk on their own after 3 years.

God's Word rings true. *"Then Jesus said to the disciples, "Have faith in God. I tell you the truth, you can say to this mountain, 'May you be lifted up and thrown into the sea,' and it will happen. But you must really believe it will happen and have no doubt in your heart. I tell you, you can pray for anything, and if you believe that you've received it, it will be yours. But when you are praying, first forgive anyone you are holding a grudge against, so that your Father in heaven will forgive your sins, too."* (Mark 11:22-25)

As Proverbs 3: 5-6 KJV says, *"Trust in the Lord with all thine heart; and lean not unto thine own understanding. In all thy ways acknowledge him, and he shall direct thy paths."*

I WAS NEVER AFRAID

By Deacon Joyce Chandler

In 1982, I had breast surgery. I was 33 years old and had recently accepted Jesus Christ as my Lord and Savior; but, I was confused. I had spent the first 9 years of my life living with my grandmother in Bushwood, Maryland in St. Mary's County. My grandmother was Catholic, a faith that believes in the practice of private confessions of sins to a priest and praying to Mary, Jesus' mother. As a new Christian, I didn't understand the full meaning of Jesus. The day of outpatient surgery at the Washington Hospital Center in the District of Columbia, I was prepped for surgery and then placed in a holding area with three other people. I began singing "Amazing Grace" and reciting the 23rd Psalm.

When I was taken to the surgical room to be moved from my bed to the operating table, it seemed I never touched the table. I felt the arms of the Lord holding me. After surgery, I didn't take any pain medication. The nurses couldn't understand and called the doctor, who said it was okay. The Lord took my pain away. *THANK GOD FOR JESUS!*

On October 31, 2012, I had cervical spondylosis surgery at Anne Arundel Hospital in Annapolis, that left me unable to eat or drink for four days. Doctors removed three disks from my neck and replaced them with 14 screws, a bracket and a cadaver bone. The doctor had expected to keep me hospitalized overnight, but complications forced them to keep me longer. When they finally sent me home to Landover, Maryland, I was allowed only to sip broth, eat applesauce, Jell-O, ice cream and drink whenever I could. I had to sleep sitting up in a recliner for 6 months when I came home. Even today, I can't use my shoulders to hold a phone to my ear or turn my neck around. Doctors said I did extremely well with therapy and was able to bypass rehabilitation. Again, thank God for Jesus.

Three years later, on October 5, 2015, I was diagnosed with a brain tumor at Georgetown Hospital in Washington, D.C. Weeks earlier, my husband and I were walking to the store and he asked why I walked sideways. I said, "I'm not." He said, "You are." It wasn't until a week later when I was walking alone to the store that I realized I was walking to my right. I also experienced dizziness. A series of tests by my doctor in Maryland and X-rays at Georgetown pinpointed the tumor. Though it was benign, all my hair was cut off for surgery that left me with a ball to drain the blood and 38 staples. Before I could leave the hospital, the doctors removed the ball without any pain medication. Two weeks later, the staples were removed, a process that left me feeling each painful pinch. Again, I could not take pain medication. I thank God again. I am still happy and have a joyous attitude. God was right there with me. I never was afraid.

On December 18, 2017, doctors discovered my nerves were wrapped around my spinal cord. Also, the area around my spinal cord was black from arthritis. In this condition, I would sometimes wake up from sleep and couldn't move. So, I had a spinal lumbar fusion operation, again at Anne Arundel Hospital. During the surgery, doctors had to unravel the nerves, scrape off the deteriorated part of my spine and then fuse the disks to pack around a rod and screws down my back. It took 2 years for total recovery from this surgery. Sometimes my right leg is affected and begins to swell. The doctors say I must eventually have another surgery, but I know God is on my side; I am believing Him for my healing. I will make it.

I had no fear during any of my surgeries because I felt the presence of the Lord. I had some awesome doctors who could only accomplish what they did through the grace of God. I prayed and asked God to touch their heart and hands. I am blessed because I know some people with back surgeries who walk bent over. Oh, praise the Lord. I am never afraid. I can truly feel the presence of the Lord with me. I truly, truly feel Him.

SURELY GOODNESS AND MERCY SHALL FOLLOW ME

By Audrey B. Chase

Any living, breathing soul need only to look up and around to see countless signs of the Lord's goodness on earth – the brilliant sun, a blossoming flower or tree, a billowing storm cloud, the rhythmic movement of the ocean's waves, or the sheer majesty of a mountain or canyon. Undeniably, the Lord's goodness also is evident in our daily lives – in both simple and complex ways. If you are reading this, for example, you are blessed with the goodness of life itself. Other tangible signs of the Lord's goodness might include a loving family, a decent place to live, a reliable job, a loyal friend, a recuperation from an illness, a "way out of no way," and the list goes on. Ultimately, the Lord's goodness is manifested in what we experience on our journey through life and how those experiences make us feel – in the moment and in retrospect.

The range of individual experiences we have is immeasurable, of course, and vastly different from those of everyone else; so are the various ways that we understand and interpret them. As I recall the many phases and nuances of my own journey, my thoughts settle on one especially difficult time in my former workplace. In retrospect, what preceded the difficult time, I think, was a reasonably comfortable time – with well managed duties and responsibilities, positive collaborations with my executive team, challenging but just relationships with staff, periodic accolades, and great performance evaluations from departmental leadership.

I really felt like I was at the top of my game and, as a result, did not foresee anything that could break my stride. Never arrogant or audacious, I always felt grateful for the opportunity to serve in my executive position. Moreover, I was confident that *goodness* and *mercy* were, indeed, following me then and were certainly on the path to follow me all the days of my life.

Sometimes life throws you a curve ball, though, and we are faced with an unexpected interruption in our *goodness* and *mercy*. From where I stood, I found myself in the midst of a storm that would not cease, thanks to a handful of envious, self-serving individuals. After receiving an early morning phone call urging me to report to work immediately, I knew this couldn't be good. Not in my wildest dreams did I ever imagine what awaited me once I parked my car and stepped into my building.

A stranger sat outside my office waiting for me to arrive. Long story short, he was there to investigate a list of fabricated allegations designed to tarnish my character, bring down the credibility of my hard work, and destroy my reputation in the process. I could see the handwriting on the wall; somebody wanted me fired and this was the first step in that direction. The stranger politely but firmly demanded an impromptu verbal defense followed by a written report – imposed within a relatively short time frame.

At that moment, and episodically thereafter, I felt I could not breathe. I knew that I was experiencing a kind of trauma. I could not focus on anything except this humiliating experience. I felt immensely vulnerable. I could not find words to say when I needed them most. I lost interest in some things. I did not sleep well, and I cried a lot. A sea of emotions washed through me, including anger that quickly turned to shame and fear. I was overcome with anxiety as I walked around most times with knots in my stomach. How was I going to convince the stranger and others that the allegations were false?

As women often do, I talked through my trauma with a very close sistah friend and with a certain well-versed and well-respected colleague in my lifelong profession, mental health. At home, I leaned on the broad shoulders of my very supportive husband who, unbeknownst to me, called on the pastor as an intercessor. Subsequently, from the phone in my office, I gladly accepted the pastor's offer to pray with me. Most importantly, I prayed too, from many private places – like my car, my bed, my shower, my kitchen and during walks. I prayed for more *goodness* and *mercy* to follow me. I specifically asked the Lord to remove the envious, self-serving individuals from my space. I didn't want to see them or be near them. I didn't want them to hurt me anymore.

Although I can't say that I *always* trusted that the Lord would answer my prayer, He did. Not in the way I expected, but He did. Instead of moving the individuals from my workplace, He moved *me* to a different space. And, although I did not think so at the time, it was just the space I needed to heal, start over, reaffirm my value and worth, receive another opportunity to use my knowledge and skills, advance, and help others. Through this hard trial, then, He kept me in the midst of it all!

Having been connected to the power of music all my life, I relied on it to serve as a kind of self-ministry during this difficult aspect of my journey. I looked for and found reassurance in gospel music that proclaimed the *goodness* of the Lord. Whether in the privacy of my own space or with my fellow choir members at church, singing the lyrics allowed me to again feel protected, understood, and in sync with the Lord, and to keep praising the Lord through my most difficult circumstances. It was and still is so comforting to be reminded that life's battles belong *not* to us but to the Lord. Through music, I am comforted as I invite the Lord's infinite goodness into my life – allowing it to gently rest, reign, move, and rule in my heart. In the words of a song writer, "For His *goodness* and His *mercy* toward us, we offer praise!"

GOD'S COMFORT TO ME

By Dorothy Simpson Cotton

In 1982, I was in an automobile accident and suffered injuries that affected my life tremendously. I was living in Glenarden, Maryland at the time and was on the way to work at the Environmental Protection Agency (EPA) in the nation's capital. As I traveled in my Park Avenue Buick down Sheriff Road with my daughters Kathy and Carlotta in the car, I noticed a pickup truck behind me in the rear-view mirror. We were sitting behind a car that was trying to make a left turn. I could see in the mirror that the truck was speeding, headed in my direction.

I turned my head to the right as I warned my daughters to brace for the impact of a coming collision. The truck rammed into the back, pushing the trunk into the back of the car where the young ladies were sitting. Because of my warning to them, however, my daughters avoided serious injuries. My vehicle was totaled. I was injured because I had turned my head. My nerves were damaged on the right side of my body. Doctors described it as a "brain stem bruise."

The serious nature of my injuries led doctors to send me to a head injury rehabilitation center in Maine. My treatment included caring for various animals, including Turkish Angora cats that produce mohair used for sweaters. I also worked with flowers. Doctors monitored my reactions while I performed the different chores to test my mental and physical stability. These tests and others that required memorization revealed my inability to mentally retain information.

The evaluation of the doctors forced me to retire from my job at the EPA. Specialists told me I would never work again and said that I should be happy with working in my flower garden and loving my grandchildren. At that time, I had six children and four grandchildren. I had worked at the EPA for 8 years.

Through all the pain, healing, trials and tests, I never gave up. My parents had been the perfect example of perseverance. Being the oldest of six children, I watched my parents weather all sorts of life storms. They showed their faith and they taught me the importance of having a strong faith and a close relationship with the Lord, Jesus Christ.

I was determined, with my mental challenges, to regain my memory of the 23rd Psalm. It had been my comfort since age 5. I was taught this Psalm by my parents and it has carried me through moments of fear. The injuries from that accident had taken my Psalm away from me. When I returned home from the rehabilitation center, my husband was my main care provider and often prayed with me. I remember every morning sitting at the table, reading the 23rd Psalm. I would recite one line and when I went to the second line, I couldn't recall the first. One glorious day, I began to remember my 23rd Psalm.

My girls and I began taking classes together under Deacon Duncan Calcote and Rev. Ronald Crawford at First Baptist Church of Highland Park in Landover, Maryland. Even though I had problems remembering the Scriptures I had to learn, I did not give up. Rev. George Frisby, a deacon at the time, would faithfully call me to encourage me. Former First Lady Mary McCord also would call to encourage me.

Today, with my six children, I have six grandchildren and 15 great-grandchildren. The 23rd Psalm still rules in my life and remains my comfort.

WHEN THE SPIRIT MOVES

By Rev. Janie Crawford

When my son Russell left Washington, D.C. to attend Wilberforce University in Ohio, I would sit in his room at the foot of his bed and pray and meditate because I wanted the Lord to help him be successful. His bedroom became my private prayer room. I had begun to pray more because I was on a mission. I knew that only God could make a way for my son to graduate with a college degree. And, I knew that God would somehow get Russell the money he needed to pay for his education.

My confidence in God stemmed from a strong relationship I started to develop at 6 years old. I always loved going to Sunday School at the AME Zion Church at Sixth and L streets in the District of Columbia. Instead of staying for "Junior Church," I would run upstairs and listen to the preacher. To me, the preacher told stories, but adults called them sermons.

So, on April 6, 1975, an Easter night, I was praying and meditating in my "private prayer room" when I was filled with the Holy Spirit. Whenever I meditate, I have soft music playing. I was sitting there in the dark listening to a recording by the Rev. Dr. James Cleveland, a noted gospel singer, musician and composer. I began to reflect on the Lord's hand working in my life through the years.

At the end of my meditation that night, I opened my eyes and said, "I thank you Lord. If I could speak another language, I would thank you in another language." The record was almost over so I stood up with my hands above my head swaying to the music. Suddenly, a good feeling came over me. I said "hmmm, hmmm, I feel like the Spirit is moving through me." Then, suddenly my mouth opened, and I began to speak. I said "Hebrew" out loud. I then began writing a letter to my son with my finger in the palm of my other hand.

I wrote, "Go on Russell take your exam, everything is going to be all right." Then, I went to my bedroom where the radio was playing "Precious Lord, Take My Hand." That is my favorite hymn, so I started singing along with the female artist, but oddly I was not singing in English.

I was feeling so good the next morning, I decided to go to the laundromat to wash my clothes even though I owned a washer and dryer. I just wanted to get out of the house and walk. When I got to the laundromat, only one lady was in there putting clothes in the washer. When I looked clearly at her, I saw a beautiful green light above her head. That was the first time I had ever seen a light above someone's head. A few minutes later, I began talking to the lady, telling her about my experience from the prior evening. I even told her about the letter I was writing to my son in my hand. I told her how I understood what I was saying as I was writing, even though the words were not English. After telling her all about it, she said, "God has given you a gift."

After my encounter with the woman at the laundromat, I wrote my son a letter. I told him God has given me a gift. I gave the letter to my husband to mail. After he went to mail the letter, I began to feel bad because I wondered if the woman who said I had received a gift from God knew what she was talking about. I began to question whether God had given me a gift. I wondered if I was lying on God in saying He had given me a gift. I began to worry. I then thought that if I prayed and meditated on it, God would somehow let me know if I had a gift.

After praying and meditating, I became very tired. I had not received an answer. I decided to go to bed. Then, I thought that if I placed the Bible under my head, I would dream the answer to my question. I had never heard of such a thing, but the idea came to me clearly. I put the Bible under my pillow and lay my head on it. I did dream that night. I saw a waterfall. As I gazed at the waterfall, I eventually came to realize it was not water falling; it was blood. I said out loud, "That's blood!" I woke myself up.

Sunday morning came, the date was April 13. I sat up in bed, then looked at the clock. It was 4:50 a.m. My next thought was that I had not received an answer to my question. I got out of bed, stood up, raised my hands and prayed. *"Heavenly Father, will thou open thy mouth and speak concerning words to me."* I repeated these words three times. Then I asked if what I wrote my son was all right. Every time I prayed those words, I would lean over trying to hear the Lord's voice. When I realized I was still not receiving an answer, I threw up both my hands, thinking I would not receive an answer. I decided to go to the bathroom. As I was walking, I suddenly stopped and just stood there looking at the ceiling.

I began to feel a gentle upward pull on my neck. As my neck stretched, my mouth began to open, and my tongue began to move. My hands were raised in a frightened position. Then, I heard these words coming from my mouth, "It is all right!" When the word "It" was spoken, the sound was so loud my husband moved in the bed, but he did not wake up. When the last word "all right" was spoken, I could suddenly move again. I covered my mouth with my hands and ran from the room into the room where my mother slept. I was not running because I was afraid; I was running because I was happy that I had received an answer.

"Mamma, everything is going to be all right," I said. She had a surprised look on her face, but she softly said, "All right."

That night, I asked my husband, "Russell, did you hear a voice in the room this morning?"

"A voice? I hope you're not losing your mind," he said, knowing I was always in prayer for our son.

Praise the Lord, He did answer my prayer. My son made the Dean's List that trimester, and it was not his only time making it. He graduated that same week, on April 18, 1975.

May God bless you all.

AMAZING GRACE

By Dr. Sandra Edmonds Crewe

My husband, Dwight, suffered a serious stroke in 1996 while we were attending my son's football game at Largo High School. His prognosis was that he would not survive and if he did, he would likely require long-term care because of physical and mental impairments. Doctors advised that I should prepare our two sons, who were ages 15 and 24 at the time, for their dad's imminent death. My reaction to the doctor's matter-of-fact statement was, "I don't believe his life or death is in your hands."

During this time, I was completing my doctorate in social work and working full time. With this news, I would be faced with the sole responsibility for parenting and supporting the household. While these were serious challenges, my greatest concern was that my husband, at age 46, had not been saved nor had he joined a church. During the same time frame, his sister was also seriously ill. Dwight's mother, a faithful prayer warrior, prayed and asked the Lord to save both of her precious children. However, she said that if she had to lose a child, her petition was for the Lord to take her oldest and dear daughter because she was saved, but her son was not. At the time, I could not imagine such faith.

During my darkest hour, after evening hospital visits, I drove to First Baptist Church of Highland Park in Landover, Maryland and sat in the parking lot. It was my place of prayer and meditation. I fervently asked the Lord for my husband's life to be spared. On Sundays, Highland Park members also prayed with me. A group of First Baptist deacons also went to the hospital and prayed with Dwight for his acceptance of Christ and for his full recovery. Only family members were permitted in Dwight's hospital room because of his critical condition. But somehow, the deacons gained entry by saying that they were his "brothers."

As the weeks passed, Dwight gained strength. I witnessed my husband singing "Amazing Grace" with the hospital chaplain. After weeks of extensive rehabilitation, he returned to work. His faith grew during this time as did mine. After being released from the rehabilitation center, Dwight attended church the next Sunday and took the walk of faith in response to Rev. George D. Frisby's petition. My husband was baptized, at age 47, and joined our church and continues to attend regularly.

Sadly, his sister died, and he attended her funeral with his mother. Subsequently, he became a devoted caregiver for his mother until her death. Also, he is the guardian for his other sister who is in long-term care and a support system for his adult niece, the child of his deceased sister. Look at God!

I professed my faith at the age of 6 years old at First Baptist Church in Meadville, Virginia. My dad's family were founding members of the Meadville church, which is about 103 years old now. While I was faithful during my adult life, my faith had never been truly tested until my husband suffered the stroke. During this season, my faith stood the test and my church family was there for us. Grateful! Grateful! Grateful! The Scripture, Philippians 4:13 (KJV), *"I can do all things through Christ which strengtheneth me"* guided our way and continues to provide spiritual strength for both of us.

GOD WORKS THROUGH VILLAGES

By Barbara M. Davis

There is an African Proverb that says, "It takes a village to raise a child." I was truly raised by the village that included my Grandma Lucy, Grandpa Walter Moore and father, Floyd Moore. My mom, Agnes Waddy Moore, died on December 30, 1944, in Bronx, New York, when I was 6 years old. I still remember the long drive from New York to Lancaster County, Virginia, for her burial. What was my dad to do with three young girls to raise on his own? It was decided that my older sisters, Mildred and Martha, and I would stay in Virginia to be under the watchful eye of the matriarch of my mother's family, Lucy Waddy.

Part of the village team was my mother's sister, Aunt Sophia Brown, who would bring new dresses that were just for me when she visited Virginia from New York. I loved her dearly because she knew I did not always like wearing clothes that had been worn by my two older sisters. We were poor, but

I did not know or feel it. Often Aunt Sophie would visit Virginia during the annual Revival Week that began the first Sunday in August at Hartwells Baptist Church. It was during the last night of one of these revivals that I accepted Christ as my Lord and Savior. Shortly thereafter, I was baptized in a river in the area of Ottomon, Virginia. Little did I know or realize that God was preparing me, even fortifying me, for the road and a few mileposts ahead!

Of my sisters, I was the last to leave Virginia and return to New York. When Dad first came to get me, I ran into the woods and stayed until I thought he would be gone. Several years later, I finally caved in and moved to New York, mainly because Grandma Lucy became sick and I could no longer take care of her by myself. So, to New York I went, traveling from an area with segregated schools to one with predominately white schools! How do you say, "cultural shock!" I struggled a bit academically at first but achieved a high average by the time of my high school graduation five years later.

Dad remained a widower for many years but there were many women who helped nurture me along the way. I stayed with Mrs. Catherine Penn or Mae Baine sometimes after school or when Dad was away. Eventually, Dad married Mary Garnett when I was nearing the end of high school. I affectionately called her Mother Mary. She truly was my rock in my senior high school year and throughout my days at Morgan State University, the largest of Maryland's historically black colleges and universities in Baltimore. I chose to attend Morgan

State because I wanted to be in an environment that would not overlook me and give me a chance of leadership. I did not get those opportunities at the predominately white Amityville High School in New York. In fact, I only applied to historically black colleges and universities.

I flourished at Morgan and carried a B+ average most semesters as a mathematics major. I graduated with a bachelor's degree in Mathematics in 1960, many decades before the now popular concept of STEM — science, technology, engineering, and math — would be encouraged for women and people of color. During my career, I had five jobs, but I believe I was stretched the most at M-Cubed Information Systems under President Neil Jones, also the owner. Over this time, I had numerous leadership opportunities.

When I reflect, I can see God's hand throughout my life, almost from the moment I professed my faith in Him. He put into my path all sorts of people – company presidents like Neil Jones, strong community activists like Dorothy Height and Betty Shabazz, people of faith like the Rev. Dr. Yvonne Felton, a techno wiz like Cheryl Hickmon, and a young trailblazing scientist like Jennifer Stimpson These people sharpened me with their new ideas. However, God gets all the glory!

I am still in the growth mode, being challenged to continue to learn and to grow. I chair the Budget Committee at First Baptist Church of Highland Park in Landover, Maryland, and

I write grants for a nonprofit organization that helps victims of crime, work that has sharply increased the group's budget to finance greater work.

The Master took me from a two-room house in Virginia to a middle-class home in Prince George's County, Maryland. My humble beginnings helped me develop a humble servant's heart that wants to give back from the blessings that God has given me.

"I can do all things through Christ who strengthens me."
(Philippians 4:13 KJV)

THIS IS THE AIR I BREATHE

By Rev. Costella H. Davis

Breathing is something that many people take for granted. But let's suppose you had an issue with breathing. I know that as a singer, I once took breathing for granted. I was able to hold notes for long periods of time and had a vocal range that encompassed the high C of a soprano. I have been singing since I was 4 years old, mostly imitating singers like Kate Smith, Jim Neighbors, Leontine Price and Mahalia Jackson. Strange for a young girl, I know, but the music that these celebrities sang brought a calm and a peace to my spirit.

I was one of 13 children born to Alberry and Wilhelmina Hunt Sr. in Bucksport, South Carolina. They were the best parents in the world and encouraged me as I developed my skills as a singer. I sang my first solo when I was about 8 years old at my home church, Salem African Methodist Episcopal. In ninth grade, I sang "Summertime" from Porgy and Bess at a school assembly at Conway High School. My classmates and family were very happy and surprised that I could sing the aria with such ease.

At Whittemore High School, I sang in the choir, where Ms. Louise Floyd, the director, noticed my talent and began to help me understand music theory. As schools integrated in 1970 in South Carolina, a new choir director, Joseph Hester, encouraged me to join a group of six singers called "The Sixteens." My parents had to agree because rehearsals were after school and I didn't have a way to get home. But, God made a way and the director or his son would drive me home. I won each state singing competition that I entered during high school and in college. To God be the glory.

I had a desire to become an opera singer because I was told that was the type of music that best suited my voice. Mr. Hester wanted me to take voice lessons and actually paid a local voice teacher to train me and help familiarize me with the piano. While I thank God for the director's kindness and interest in me, I now know that this was an assignment from God. Praise the Lord!

When I completed high school, I wanted to go to college as the first in my family of 13, but my parents couldn't afford it. By this time, my relationship with God was strong. I joined church before my 13th birthday, although I always had a yearning for Christ and a deep love for God. It seemed the Lord has always been all over my life and I intuitively knew He was looking out for me. So, I left my home three days after graduating from high school and moved to Maryland with my sister, Patricia, and her family. I met Allen S. Hammond III, a noted Doctor of Music, and his wife Dorothy, at Randall Memorial United Methodist in the Northeast part of the District of Columbia. The couple welcomed me into their home, and under their wings; just like it is spoken of in Psalm 91, they cared for me. One day, the couple took me to The Catholic University of America to sing for some of the professors there. Little did I know, I was doing an entrance audition for the Dean of Music, the head of the Vocal Faculty and the Opera Workshop coach. After waiting around for about an hour, they came out of the hall and said I could start school on the Tuesday after Labor Day.

I graduated from Catholic University in May 1981 and was selected from all the singers in the music school to sing the National Anthem with orchestral accompaniment. This was quite an honor. After earning my bachelor's degree, I sang solos at many concerts in the Washington Metropolitan area as well as in South Carolina. I sang operas while in school but never got that big break I wanted. What I realized, however, is that becoming an operatic singer wasn't what God had for me. I had worked for several federal agencies since moving to the area and retired in 2012 as a senior contract specialist with a "Yankee White Clearance" level and an unlimited Contracting Officer's warrant. I give God all the glory, honor and praise for all my achievements. Yet, He still is not finished with me.

My father died on January 2, 1996, just a few months shy of his 70th birthday. Before then, my siblings and I had been traveling home each weekend to help our mother care for Dad at home. Also, about seven months before his death, in June

1995, I accepted Jesus Christ as my Lord and Savior. Three to four weeks before he died, my sister Teresa and I gave our jobs notice and returned home. I found myself up many nights reading the Bible and singing to my dad while everyone else was sleeping. The last thing I read to my father was his favorite Bible passage, the 23rd Psalm. Also, during this time, I was feeling very sluggish and out of sorts, but I just chalked it up to circumstances.

After I returned to work, I found it difficult to walk the Navy Yard halls. My breathing was labored, and I just couldn't keep up with coworkers. I had a sister who died from a heart attack as a complication of sarcoidosis. My symptoms made me think that maybe I had it too. Another sister had been diagnosed with the inflammatory disease that affects multiple areas of the body but, praise the Lord, she got pregnant with her second child, and it went into remission.

What I learned later was that I suffered from pulmonary hypertension. I asked the doctor what it was, and he said, "Well, if you don't get treated for it, and follow my orders explicitly, you will die." I started to laugh, and I said, "What are you talking about?" He told me that I needed to have oxygen 24/7, 365 days and for how long he wasn't certain. I laughed harder and louder. My sister told the doctor that I was in shock.

I had been singing since I was 4 years old, throwing all kinds of air away and just doing it for fun. Now, I was being told my body could not produce enough air to keep me alive on its own. I was trying to think, how will this affect my life, especially my job and my marriage. My husband, Cleveland, and I were about to adopt a baby. The doctor said adoption was out because I wouldn't be able to take care of myself, let alone a baby. I could not climb stairs or walk for long distances. I had to be careful about lifting things as well. My entire life was changed in that moment. But thanks be to God, I knew that my Father cared for me and He proved it.

Within a few days of my diagnosis, God sent three complete strangers to let me know that this condition would not be forever, and I was not going to die anytime soon. The oxygen company came to my house to deliver a big stationary oxygen tank and several small tanks, as well as a "concentrator" that used distilled water. When I went to work, I had to explain to my boss my need for the equipment in our office. My colleagues called a meeting and agreed to allow liquid oxygen in our workspace so that I could continue the job. Also, I got parking right at our door. Eventually, however, our command closed and relocated to San Diego, California. Other job prospects fell through because of the oxygen tank. It was also during this time that God started to call me to ministry. I had my own closed off cubicle and people would come in and unburden themselves as I listened, consoled and prayed with them.

As time went on, I assisted several of my colleagues in finding jobs while I was still left behind. Then one day God smiled on me. I was chosen from a list of candidates, sight unseen, just because I was from the great state of South Carolina. I continued to climb the ladder of success in contracting and

I continued to sing while wearing my oxygen. Years were passing, and I kept working, going to church, being involved in different ministries and praying. God is so good to us and sometimes we just need to stop and enjoy it, breathing in the air He supplies for us daily. I took air for granted until I couldn't make enough to sustain my life. But God never left me, nor did He forsake me.

I kept wearing the oxygen as my career advanced and finally, I was told I could reduce the liters of oxygen that I was using. Then, I was allowed to cut down on how often I used it. Finally, after about nine years, I was set free from my tanks and the concentrator. I testified about it and before I knew it, I took off running in my church. Can you image that? I was overcome with the goodness of the Lord.

My husband and I were able to adopt our beautiful daughter, Chelsea Abigail, and we had eight wonderful years raising her together before he died on December 22, 2013, a week before our 23rd wedding anniversary. We should never take anything for granted; we should bless the Lord and thank Him as often as we can for His loving kindness towards us. Breathing is such an easy thing when there are no problems but when there are problems, you can feel that pull for dear life. God, I thank you for the air that I breathe, and more than that, that you loved me enough to take me through this trial in my life. I pray that someone else who might be tied to an oxygen tank can see beyond the forest to the revelation of a new life.

PRESSING TOWARD THE MARK

By Chekesha Duncan

Martin Luther King Jr. Day 2017, I sat across from the man whom I had shared my heart and soul with for 21 years. I listened intently as he told me he wanted a divorce and had renewed his relationship with his ex. I cringed when he told me he had never loved me, and she had his heart. My life changed in that moment forever.

The man I had met so many years before as a young 24-year-old girl had crushed me and made me question everything I ever believed about love. One week later, I lost my job, so in addition to the loss of my marriage, I was now unemployed. Three weeks later, I moved out of the space in Severn, Maryland I had shared with my husband and two sons, who were aged 16 and 11 at the time, and into the basement of my best friend's home in Beltsville, 30 minutes away. My world had shifted; I was completely lost.

Leaving behind my boys was one of the hardest decisions I have ever made in my life. I wrestled with staying and being consumed with external activities or leaving and becoming healthy and whole. This choice often left me in tears. What woman leaves her kids, right? That first night I cried in anger and pain and prayed that things would go back to 'normal.' It was then that I had my first true encounter with God. I heard with such clarity and conviction, "Let Go." Nothing more than "let go." I slept soundly for the first time in weeks after hearing that message.

That night I dreamed of a cartoon I often see on social media of a little girl holding a torn and tattered teddy bear and Jesus holding a new bigger bear behind His back. I would love to say I knew what He wanted me to do but that would be a lie. Now, I spent a lifetime in church because that was what a good woman did, right? I served and took classes, but I didn't have a relationship with God and never understood what that meant until I had reached out to grasp and there was nothing there to hold on to. It seems nothing fit any longer, nothing could feed me or quench my thirst.

Over the next year, my position at rock-bottom became my solid foundation to rebuild my life. This journey has not been easy. Day by day I seek God earnestly. I fall short daily, but my mantra is "Every second, every minute, every hour, I choose You, Lord." I've learned to "Trust in the Lord with all my heart and lean not unto my own understanding." (Proverbs 3:5 KJV) I realized my self-esteem was non-existent long before the end of my marriage and that led me to therapy.

My favorite Bible chapter is Psalm 139, where I am reminded that if God could love me enough to know me in my mother's womb, then who am I not to love myself. Oh, to be loved like this, my heart sings when I allow Him in. My visual cue has been an onion and each layer I peel away brings me closer to God. There are days where I feel the sting of the onion in my eyes and know that my peace and joy were so worth the pain.

The year 2018 was filled with challenges but in March of that year, I was baptized and truly gave my life to Christ. I thought that if I "studied and showed myself approved" things would magically fall into place. I believed that if I lived in love, my troubles would magically disappear. It was as if I believed God would wave a magic wand to make it all better. So, I returned to the Scripture Proverbs 3:5 and realized that the medical challenges I had endured gave me the strength to persevere and truly understand what it means to trust in the Lord.

I know that there is a promise if I keep pressing toward the mark. I used to laugh when people gave me those Scriptures because they were just words. How could this possibly be of use when my marriage is falling apart, and I am sad and lonely living in someone's basement away from my boys? This road has not been easy, and I don't have all the answers, but each challenge that comes my way, I can smile at my Heavenly Father and count it all joy.

I have finally moved into my own apartment; my divorce has become final. I am learning to forgive as I count each small victory and thank the Holy Spirit for giving me love, joy and peace.

THE UNEXPECTED GIFT OF CHANGE

By Chekesha Duncan

She watched as he blended his world
accepting hand me downs and second guesses.
It's no wonder he settled for less than his hopes and dreams.
She accepted that he relegated his rhythms
to a flow that fed his flaws
He danced along even though he wasn't moved by the music
He longed for a beat that matched his heart's desire.
She allowed excuses that were chiseled
in the gravestones of regret
And when blame hugged the ground like a toxic mist
she filled with dew that left her soaked with weighted sorrow
She paid the price for believing in tomorrow
even when the account was negative today.
So when she gave and gave and gave
allowing him to overdraft her as she invested in him
she prayed that bitterness would not become her cloak
Serving herself to someone who couldn't understand
the wealth of her being, trading rubies for rubble
he was content in playing with less than
so she honored his withdrawal
and invested in a commodity that doesn't depreciate
She valued the self love and created residual wealth
sowing seeds that generated prosperity for years to come
She found value in the Son rising
and never questioned if the check was good
Giving became second nature
without question she knew
that the price had been paid, all was forgiven
and the change was more than enough for more.

"I know how to live on almost nothing
or with everything
I have learned the secret of living in every situation,
whether it is with a full stomach or empty,
with plenty or little.
For I can do everything through Christ,
who gives me strength"

~ Philippians 4:12-13

Chapter Two

Contributors E through K

"For I can do everything through Christ,

who gives me strength."

~ Philippians 4:13

THE PICTURE

By Carolyn Ellerbe

I believed living in a garden apartment in Northeast Washington, D.C., with a courtyard view, was the right fit for me. It was there I met my next-door neighbor, Joyce, who was single and traveled a lot on company business and we became friends. When she was on travel, I would water her plants and collect her Sunday *Washington Post* newspaper that was left at her apartment door.

One evening while I was eating dinner, my brother Dennis, who was about 26 or 27 years old at the time, stopped by to visit me after spending the day applying for full-time employment. I just knew that having a college degree from North Carolina Central University would make it easy for Dennis to find a good-paying job. However, after three months of interviews, he was getting tired of job hunting and hearing employers say, *"I will call you later with our decision."*

While having dinner together, I told Dennis about an advertisement I remember seeing in my neighbor's newspaper a week earlier. The FBI was accepting applications to fill 500 open positions, but the deadline was fast approaching. It is funny how things can happen. You see, I am not a person who reads newspapers. I might browse through the Style Section or flip through the newspaper, and then I am done.

But the FBI advertisement caught my attention while I was flipping pages. I pulled that issue from the newspaper pile I'd collected from my neighbor's door and gave it to my brother to read. Dennis decided to spend the night with me because it was getting late. The next morning, he went to the local library, got the 10-page FBI application, and completed the questionnaire. But he needed a headshot photo. Everything had to be submitted within 48 hours since the article had been in a week-old newspaper.

As I stated earlier, I don't read newspapers. Also, I don't like taking pictures. But, I told Dennis that I had purchased a one-step camera that would output a hard copy of the picture within minutes. Unfortunately, I had used all the film in the pack, and it sat empty on a shelf in my closet. I told Dennis that I would pray and ask God for His help. Dennis just smiled.

That night, believing God really does answer prayers, I asked Him to help me get a picture of my brother so we could mail the application that morning. I awoke early the next day and began looking around my bedroom. I started to talk to God saying *"God you said you would answer one's prayers if we prayed in faith and believed in Your Word, which I do. So please help me with the problem."*

While lying in bed, I realized that I could no longer hear familiar sounds inside nor outside my apartment. At that moment, it felt like an ocean wave had come over my body, starting at my feet and traveling up to my neck, my body seemed paralyzed. I could, however, still think and speak. This was when I heard a voice talking to me, but I could not understand the language.

I said, *"God, I hear You, but I don't know what you are saying."*

Then, I heard Him say, *"Get up in the morning, get the camera and take the picture. Tell him to be encouraged. He will get the position."*

Just as that ocean wave came over my body, it left from my neck back down and over my feet. At once, all the familiar sounds returned, and I regained my ability to move. I could not believe what had just happened. It took me a while to understand it all.

I could not go back to sleep, so I got up very early and woke up Dennis to tell him what had just happened. Again, he just smiled and said, *"There are no films in the camera, we checked, remember?"*

My response? *"Yes, we did, but God said, 'get the camera and take a picture."*

I took the camera from the closet, and lo and behold, there was one film left. ONLY GOD!! Just know that God does answer prayers — BIG OR SMALL. God does speak personally to you through his Word, the Holy Bible.

Fast forward, a year later, my brother Dennis became an FBI agent and has worked for the agency for more than 10 years. Won't HE do it?! This made a big difference in my brother's life and mine. Dennis W. Moody is now pastor of Sharon Missionary Baptist Church in Big Island, Virginia.

As for me, I will continue to praise and thank God for the life He has blessed me with.

IT'S MOVING TIME, PRAISE THE LORD!

By Sharon Everett-Hardin

It was the summer of 1989 after the Fourth of July when the Lord spoke to me that it was time for a change. I had been working at a department store for almost five years in Suffolk, Virginia and living with my parents. Within the next six months, I began to pay off bills and save money. I made a decision to quit my job and move to Maryland in January 1990. I informed the store manager that my last day was going to be after the store inventory, on January 18. When I began to tell family and friends of my decision about moving, everyone's questions were: "Why?" and "Do you have a job?" My answers were: "It is time to move" and "No, I do not have a job." I told them that I believed that the Lord would provide.

On January 28, my last Sunday at my home church, Canaan Baptist Church in Suffolk, the organist, Greg, sang a song that he dedicated to me, titled "Look it's Right there in the Word of God." It truly blessed my heart. While saying my goodbyes at church, it was a very sad moment, but many were very happy for me. After church, some of my family members came over to my parent's house for dinner and to watch the Super Bowl. The next day, I knew I would be getting on the road to Forestville, Maryland, in Prince George's County. It was a cold and cloudy Monday morning and the forecast was calling for snow. I knew that it was time to leave. My parents gave me their blessings and prayed with me. My mother gave me her Bible, which I still have today, and told me to read Psalm 128. My Aunt Thelma came over to the house before I left to wish me well. My white 1987 Skyhawk Buick was all packed and ready for the trip.

I arrived in Forestville to stay with a college friend from Norfolk State University, Pam, and her 2-year-old daughter, Lauren. Within two days, I began to look for a job and go on job interviews. The Lord blessed me to find a job within two weeks. I started work at CT Corp. in Washington, D.C. on February 17, 1990. I am truly thankful that over the years I have had other job opportunities and that the Lord has provided and will continue to provide as I stepped out on faith and believe on His Word.

"Blessed is everyone that feareth the Lord; that walketh in his ways. For thou shalt eat the labour of thine hands: happy shalt thou be, and it shall be well with thee. Thy wife shall be as a fruitful vine by the sides of thine house: thy children like olive plants round about thy table. Behold, that thus shall the man be blessed that feareth the Lord. The Lord shall bless thee out of Zion: and thou shalt see the good of Jerusalem all the days of thy life. Yea, thou shalt see thy children's children, and peace upon Israel." (Psalm 128 KJV)

A CRYING CHILD TRAPPED IN AN ADULTS BODY!

By Robin Fields

I was born on July 16, 1969 in Cheverly, Maryland to the late Rodney "Rocky" Hunter and Theresa Elaine Stewart. I can remember when my father would rob banks and come to my house in Capitol Heights in his pink Cadillac and give all the kids change, and me dollar bills. My father eventually was arrested and sent to prison when I was 10 years old. These are some of my earliest memories.

My mother was strung out on heroin and died when I was 13 years old. That was one of the worse days of my life. It hurt me to my soul that I had lost my mom. I lost faith in God. After her death, I moved in with my grandmother in Seat Pleasant, Maryland. She never really liked me because her man, at the time, tried twice to molest me. I lost my virginity at 14 years old with that same man. It also was at age 14 when my first love's mother, Mrs. Ella Hall, now deceased, told me I was God's chosen one and that He was going to take me through some things to test my faith. Mrs. Hall would conduct Bible study in her home before allowing her children to play outside. I tended to be the only one who stayed inside to read God's Word, which at that time was very empowering to me.

In the following years, God blessed me with two beautiful daughters, Lorell and Lanay. My grandmother died when I was 18. Shortly after that, I met Warren, a wonderful man who helped me raise my daughters. We married on my 21st birthday, and together we had Warren Jr. and Latisha. Unfortunately, we divorced in 2001. Three years later, in 2004, I was living in Annapolis addicted to crack cocaine and working for the Maryland Highway Department. While on that job, I met and married an apostolic minister, but the marriage didn't last.

On February 3, 2018, my father, Rocky, died and left me devastated because I felt he was the only person on earth who really loved me. Despite all the ups and downs in my life, I still read God's Word and continued to worship in church on a regular basis. Months later, a series of events occurred that left me feeling like I was God's version of Job. But, I thank God that He blessed me with four grandchildren, Jahiem and Jaylan, and Reign and Paige. Also, I earned my high school diploma in June 2017. PRAISE GOD FROM WHOM ALL BLESSINGS FLOW!!

Surviving it all, I am now on fire for the God that I serve! I accepted God and His Son, Jesus, into my life, with the Holy Spirit covering me, the day I joined First Baptist Church of Highland Park (the City on the Hill) under the dynamic leadership of my pastor, the Rev. Dr. Henry P. Davis III. I had never danced before but every time I think about how God saved me, I can't stay still. He guides me in everything I do and provides for me. I witness about Jesus everywhere I am. I witness on my Facebook page and in my community. God provides for me and gives me enough to share with others.

I am not ashamed to praise His name because I know what God has brought me through. I am full of joy and peace, and I promised to serve Him forever.

A NEW LEASE ON LIFE

By Candice C. Floyd

At first, I thought it was a death sentence. Yet, when I first was diagnosed with a cerebral aneurysm, I began to realize the importance of slowing down and extracting myself from unnecessary demands. It was then my daily life became more fulfilling.

This condition I had, as the doctor explained, is caused by a weakened blood vessel in the brain that balloons and fills with blood. Few people get warnings with a cerebral aneurysm, much less live through it. But glory to God, I survived two cerebral aneurysm surgeries within six months. I consider myself a walking and talking miracle because not only did I survive, but also after each surgery, I had a short recovery time, with no lasting residual effects. Hallelujah!

My journey began in August 2017 when I visited my primary care physician for an annual physical. I had been seeing this doctor regularly for the past 15 years, so she is familiar with my personal and family health history. During the last exam, I mentioned that my mother had died in her sleep five months earlier, in March. Hearing this news, the doctor insisted I get an MRI as a precaution.

My mother's family has a history of aneurysms: Four of my maternal aunts had aneurysms when they were in their 40s; two of the women died immediately of their brain trauma, while two suffered severe strokes. In addition, two of my mother's brothers suffered head injuries and induced brain traumas. One uncle was 12 years old when he was struck in the head during a baseball game; he died soon after the injury. The second uncle was involved in a fight as an adult, suffered a stroke and walked with a cane the remainder of his life.

My MRI results came in and my doctor left me a voicemail; a cerebral aneurysm was located approximately two inches behind my left eye. When I heard the voicemail, I could only think the worse. In retrospect, I should have realized that if the test results were a dire emergency, the doctor would have instructed me to go straight to a hospital emergency unit. Despite the voicemail, I was still feeling physically fine and had no symptoms. Typically, the ailment carries such symptoms as frequent headaches, blurred vision, weakness or numbness. However, I was feeling more physically fit because I had been increasing my physical activity and eating healthier.

Up until the diagnosis, I had been going through life as always — in total busyness. I am married with a 7-year-old son who attends a charter school and has played soccer, then baseball, and now Tae Kwan Do. I work full time at a college library and teach English courses at the same college two evenings a week and on Saturdays. I am also a freelance writer.

At one time, I was an alumni board member of my alma mater, the University of Maryland in College Park, where I was responsible for social media content. I also wrote, edited, and distributed a newsletter for the local Boys and Girls Club, for which my son played sports. Finally, I had been deeply involved with the care of my parents all my adult life and worked more intensively with my father when he could no longer live with me and moved to a nursing home.

While I was fine physically, the thought of an aneurysm took up a lot of mental space. I was distracted and only partially engaged with all my projects, which resulted in some missteps with everyone. I had just started to teach a new semester when I heard the doctor's voicemail message. My students suffered the brunt of my mental angst and their assignment deadlines were rescheduled several times. I joined an anxiety group that constantly reminded me that Jesus talked against worry. I struggled to remain faithful and remember that God is in control. Still, I worried at times.

My first detailed angiogram was a month after the MRI. The procedure took 45 minutes as the doctors ran a small tube from the main artery in my left leg up to my brain, where they shot contrast ink and took snapshots of my veins to get a clearer photo of the aneurysm. The goal of this procedure was to determine treatment options. I had to stay conscious for the entire procedure and remain in recovery for four hours to ensure no clots formed before I went home. I was forced to take additional time off from work, although doctors had expected me to return to work right after the procedure.

The surgery took place in the middle of October 2017, after another angiogram was performed. The surgery was extremely successful, and I was able to leave the hospital the next day. Unlike the initial angiogram, I experienced no light-headedness and needed less recovery time.

Little did I know that my ordeal wasn't over. Less than two weeks after returning to work, my father suffered a life-threatening trauma while in the hospital for a routine test. The impact of the trauma forced my family to decide to remove my father from life support; he subsequently passed away. His funeral was held the Monday after Thanksgiving. Then three months later, three days before her birthday, my father's sister also died. Like my mother, she too died in her sleep.

Just when I felt like I was getting back to a normal routine, in March 2018, months after my initial surgery, an ambulance rushed me to a hospital because another small aneurysm had formed and burst. I underwent emergency surgery and spent three weeks in the hospital's intensive care unit.

I know God spared me to be a witness to others, especially the students I teach. At the end of each semester, I share personal details as a part of a larger conversation on how these young people should remain resilient throughout their educational journey. One of my favorite Scriptures has always been Matthew 6:25-34, when Jesus tells his disciples that they should not worry and notes that if God cares for birds and flowers, so will He care for us. The ordeal helped me slow down and reevaluate how I spend the time that He has granted me. As a result, I now concentrate on activities that cultivate more value such as spending time with my family.

DISABLED DETERMINATION

By Destiny E. Floyd

I have been a good student academically since starting elementary school. I always had a desire to be a good student. I earned good grades and overall, I was a good kid. However, I was presented with some challenges along the way and to get these great academic results I had to overcome some medical disabilities, particularly Sickle Cell Disease. Sickle cell is a chronic medical condition that landed me in the hospital seven to eight times a year up to my ninth grade in high school.

I was physically unable to do things and many times unable to walk. I missed countless days of school. I wanted to be normal — to have a normal life. I was only 2 or 3 years old when I started my frequent trips to the hospital. I just remember that my mom Jennifer would pray for me whenever I was in a pain crisis. When she was finished, I would say "Amen," but I would still be in pain. I always believed my mom when she said I would feel better – just believe God will make me feel better. Whenever I was forced to stay home from school, I continued to do my schoolwork. My sickle cell had my body, but it didn't have my mind. I was determined!

Life with sickle cell has been challenging, but I maintain my determination! I can remember missing ballet recitals, holidays, swimming, playing in the snow and fun events, or just going outside because I was not feeling well. Sickle cell affected me a lot, but it never defined me. Recently, I was diagnosed with yet another medical challenge. When I found out about my diagnosis, I was sad. "Why me?" I was in the ninth or 10th grade and my mom prayed again, and I said, "Amen." She encouraged me in the doctor's office that day and reminded me that God is still in control. Just like God has allowed me to have the normal life that I wanted, she reminded me that God would work out this new medical diagnosis in my favor, and he has done just that. I believe that God looks out for me.

I have my sickle cell under control with no hospitalizations in three years. I believe God has prepared me for the battles to come in my future. Children's National Hospital in Washington, D.C. was amazed that I was still performing academically at a high level, but they said, "my determination and desire to be a good student pushes me not to fall behind in my classes and maintain my honor roll status." Thinking back, my diagnosis fueled my determination! I don't re-member when I joined First Baptist Church of Highland Park in Landover, Maryland, because I was very young. I do remember prayers from my mom, my nana, my aunts, and people in my church when I reflect over my life.

I know that my disabilities did not hurt me, they helped me and empowered me to be the best student and person I could possibly be. Even if I fell short, I knew I could still succeed in school. I have worked as president of our church's Ju-nior Missionary Ministry, completed my Silver Award in Girl Scouts, became the Sickle Cell Poster Child for "Faces of Our Children," and worked as a counselor-in-training at Sickle Cell Camp. Also, I have served as a Student Govern-ment Association (SGA) representative and maintained my National Honor Society status since my 10th grade year of high school.

I'm going to college this year with my disabilities and I thank God that I can go with the determination to succeed. I de-cided a long time ago that victory was mine if I was willing to fight for it. Yes, I have disabilities, but I'm determined that those disabilities will not define my life. I'm thankful for so many things in my life. I'm thankful for my parents, my nana, my family and I'm thankful that my mom has prayed for me all my life and introduced me to the Lord.

I believe in God and I believe that Jesus died for the sins of the world. I'm thankful that God gave me a heart for missions, and a heart to help people. I'm still learning about God and what God means to me, but because of God, I can live my best, blessed life! I'm ready for what's next and I trust God to see me through what's next.

MY LIFE CONTINUES

By Jennifer Floyd

I started writing my testimony on January 18, 2005. As I sat and tried to briefly explain my Christian experience, I didn't know where to start. All my life, I felt as though I have known the Lord. When I was young, I remember sitting in church with other children, talking and playing as kids do — I suppose. Then, I just didn't do it anymore; I started listening to the Word of God, really listening. I started to realize in my early teens that it shouldn't matter who was preaching in the pulpit or teaching the Sunday School lessons, or what choir was singing. The Word of God is the only thing that is important. I realized then that I should follow along when the preacher quoted Scriptures because I should know for myself just what the Word was saying to me!

When in high school, I was baptized but found myself rededicating my life to Christ several times until I realized that my walk with Christ was my walk with Christ and I didn't have to keep going down to the front for "altar call" to rededicate my life. I realized that nobody is perfect, not even me, and that my goal was to strive to be Christ *like*. The only *perfect* anything is Christ, so I understood that I would always come up short. I have talked about Christ with people, shared information about my life, and God's love for people. Over the years, people have come to me, seeing in me what I didn't see in myself. I love God's people — those who have accepted Christ as Lord and Savior — and I love sharing messages from His Word, what we call *planting the seeds.* Christians believe that when we take such steps to tell others about Christ, the Lord will ultimately work in that person's life to get him or her to believe as we do. Our calling is to share Christ and to let our walk be our light.

At my church, the First Baptist Church of Highland Park in Landover, Maryland, my mom, Lonnie M. Ebron, my granddaddy, William A. Ebron, and the late Deacons Bennie Oliver and Harvey Broadie, were major influences in my life and my walk with the Lord. My mother always told me that I needed to know the Lord for myself, and have a relationship with the Lord for me, not for her. Christ was the best gift my mother could have given me. I am a believer and I know that I know that I know that I can do nothing without Christ; and I can do all things through Christ who strengthens me! Wow, almost 14 years later and more than 50 years old, my testimony has not changed, but I have — in good ways.

I'm still on *the battlefield for the Lord.* I'm still sharing Christ. I'm still giving myself as service for the Lord. A preacher once said in a sermon, "you don't need to know the entire Bible, but you should have one Scripture that could be your lifeline." I don't know the entire Bible, but I do have many Scriptures that are etched into my heart and soul. My life is a witness before God, and what I do and or have done, and will continue to do with my life is a testament to God's saving grace over my life. I know God is not finished with me because Jeremiah 29:11 (NIV) says: *"For I know the plans I have for you,"* declares the Lord, *"plans to prosper you and not to harm you, plans to give you hope and a future."*

All I can do is keep my eyes on the prize, which is JESUS, and enjoy the ride! Just call me: Jennifer "Get Excited" Floyd.

THE LORD KEEPS BLESSING ME

By Odessa Burnette Gatewood

I have traveled a miraculous and adventurous journey, trusting in God every step of the way. I look forward to the dawn of every new day and its unfolding and its maturing, knowing there is room for spiritual growth and an additional opportunity to spread God's *Morning Glory* (my suggested spiritual name by brother, Don). Some of my most pivotal evidence of God's grace, mercy and blessings are described below:

Aching Legs. From about the age of two until I started first grade, my mother, Helen Bernice, prayed for me daily because of intense, constant and unexplained pains in my legs. She rubbed my legs day and night. The love and devotion of my mother and her avid faith in the power of God healed my aching legs. I was able to enjoy life without pain and able to participate in the physical and fun activities that young children love and look forward to. *"And the prayer of faith shall save the sick, and the Lord shall raise him up; and if he has committed sins, they shall be forgiven." "Confess your faults one to another, and pray one for another, that ye may be healed. The effectual fervent prayer of a righteous man availeth much."* (James 5:15-16 KJV)

Third Degree Grease Burns on Right Leg and Foot. I was burned badly in the early 1960s when my mother was pregnant with my brother, Don. As she opened the oven door to remove food she was preparing for a late dinner, my hand accidentally touched the handle of the pan and the sizzling hot grease poured down on my right leg and foot. I was wearing blue jeans, which made the burn worse because the pants clung to my leg. I had never experienced such agonizing pain. My mother applied home remedies for relief but took me to the family doctor the next morning. The doctor wrapped my leg in a cast-like covering that I wore for a few weeks. I was a bit despondent following the incident and not excited about attending school. The care and encouragement of my mother, along with the love of family and God, healed me and restored my confidence. *"He heals the brokenhearted and binds up their wounds."* (Psalm 147:3 NIV)

Ruptured Appendix. In 1968, when I was 16 years old and living in Warren County, I suffered severe abdominal pain that escalated within a few hours. I was nauseous and vomiting and literally unable to walk or sit up. During two appointments, a physician diagnosed my condition as sprained stomach muscles. But, after more intense pain, my mother and grandmother, Hattie Pearl, literally lifted me to the car and took me to a different doctor. I had become very dizzy with blurred vision, was extremely weak and in too much pain to walk or balance myself. During this visit, the doctor correctly diagnosed my condition as a ruptured appendix. Because possibly life-threatening, I was immediately admitted to Maria Parham Hospital in Henderson, North Carolina for emergency surgery.

My appendix had been ruptured for a couple of days and infection had rapidly spread throughout my abdomen. As explained by the doctor, the misdiagnosis almost caused my death. After a few weeks under the doctor's care, and with the love and care of family, I recovered. God touched my body and healed me completely. The excitement of returning to school, driving a school bus, and participating in school and community activities brought much happiness to my life. *"And the God of all Grace, who called you to his eternal Glory in Christ, after you have suffered a little while, will himself restore you and make you strong, firm and steadfast."* (1 Peter 5:10 NIV)

Sickness During Pregnancy (Hyperemesis Gravidarum). In 1970, when I was pregnant with my son, Anthony (Tony), I was lethargic and languid almost every day.

I gained only eight pounds throughout this special pregnancy. My dear sister, Goldie, and I shared an apartment in Washington, D.C. at the time. She did whatever she could to make life comfortable for me. After the birth of my amazing and beloved Tony, we relocated to North Carolina to live with my mother and father (Willie). They both were very supportive, kind, loving, generous, patient, self-sacrificing and reassuring. My sweet and protective brothers June, Eric, and Don kept times upbeat and fascinating. My fourth brother, Travis, whom I later learned about, was also accepted by our family. He too is a sweet and kind brother, and I thank God he entered our lives.

My paternal grandparents, John Henry and Hattie Pearl, and their children were extremely helpful by babying sitting Tony while I worked. Tony and I were incredibly blessed. My dad helped me to get a job at Belk-Leggett shortly after my return to North Carolina. Today, Tony and his wife, Jo'Mesha , have three talented daughters, Joyous, Canah, and Laila-Ann. *"Every good gift and every perfect gift are from above, coming down from the Father of lights, with whom there is no variation or shadow due to change."* (James 1:17 ESV)

Automobile Accident. In the year 1983, my son, Tony, and I survived a serious car accident in Warren County that left us with multiple facial lacerations and other injuries. My family was very supportive, caring, loving, and encouraging. My friends, too, showed love and compassion as well.

To convalesce, Tony and I moved in with my parents and my brother Don's family. The undying love, care, attention, and affection given to us from them helped to give us the boost and confidence we needed to move forward after such depressing injuries. Through God's grace and mercy, Tony and I were spared, healed from both emotional and physical injuries, and given a new walk. *"Though I walk in the midst of trouble, you preserve my life."* (Psalm 138:7 NIV)

Precancerous Cell Diagnosis. In 1996 when I lived in Durham, North Carolina, I was diagnosed with precancerous cells. My faith was tested, and I realized this was not about how tough I was. This was about having the faith to know I could handle all things through Christ whom I must trust in dark times. God took my hand, and through His sustaining power, I was restored to good health and given another chance. Oh, what a happy day! *"And Jesus said unto them, Because of your unbelief: for verily I say unto you, if ye have faith as a grain of mustard seed, ye shall say unto this mountain, Remove hence to yonder place; and it shall remove, and nothing shall be impossible unto you."* (Matthew 17:20 KJV)

Throughout my journey, I have been faced with what I thought were insurmountable circumstances, but God's divine guidance has been upon me. I am happily married to Curtis Gatewood who is a multi-talented minister and social justice activist. We have an amazing daughter, Desmera,

who has a talented daughter, Everette Rose. I cannot con-
clude this testimonial without giving thanks to my maternal
grandmother, Zellah Moss Jenkins. She enjoyed helping
to keep my siblings and me beautifully dressed. This also
helped to augment our household monetary flow. The Moss
family, in general, taught us how to endure challenging situations through resilience, faith, sacrifice, and hard work.
*"We are hard pressed on every side, but not crushed; per-
plexed, but not in despair; persecuted, but not abandoned;
struck down, but not destroyed."* (2 Corinthians 4:8-9 NIV)

THE POWER OF FAITH

By Betty Bunns Gay

My life changed so dramatically 15 years ago that I almost lost my self-recognition.

It all began the night of July 22, 2003. It was late and I had been waiting for my husband to come home from his medical practice. My son, Thomas, opened the garage door to the house, yelling "call 911!"

"Something is wrong with Dad," he yelled frantically.

Thomas had arrived home and found his dad lying face down in the driveway beside his car. At first, we thought he had a heart attack. Later on, in the hospital, we were told the shocking news that my husband had been shot in the head. My son, two daughters and I left the hospital in shock and disbelief. We clung to each other in my bed when we got home. We cried ourselves to sleep. My husband Thomas died three days later on July 25, 2003.

My husband's death left my life in a daze. It was like I was floating from one day to the next. I didn't have an appetite and couldn't eat or sleep.

I found myself wishing that my mother was alive. She would be by my side to help me, I thought. Although she never quoted a favorite Bible Scripture, she often impressed upon me the importance of having faith in God. She spoke of just having *"faith the size of a mustard seed."* (Matthew 17:20 NASB) My father worked hard as a self-employed tile layer. His work involved lifting a heavy iron roller on and off the bed of a pickup truck and spending lots of time on his knees. At the end of a day's work while soaking in a tub of hot water, he sometimes would sing with deep emotion, "Down by The Riverside." It was like he had satisfaction knowing that there was the option of leaving all our cares with the Lord and being at peace. I grew up knowing the necessity of having faith in God and that I could carry my burdens to the Lord.

In 1996, a friend visited me following the death of my mother and, commenting on the Scripture *"Jesus wept"* (John 11:35 KJV), left a tract. It helped me to grieve and has since been one of my favorite Scriptures. However, the 23rd Psalm always has been my "go to" Scripture. For example, I am claustrophobic and have had MRI exams in the past where saying the Lord's Prayer and the 23rd Psalm would keep me completely still and comforted through the ordeal.

With the murder of my husband, however, I needed another power to help me survive the change in my life, even with the support of family and friends. Reaching out in faith, I asked God to help me, tell me what to do daily, give me strength to endure, and help me to carry my burden.

I kept a journal and a Bible by my bedside. When I awoke during the night, unable to sleep, I would read my Bible until I fell asleep. I recorded my thoughts and wrote daily "thank you" notes in my journal.

I found myself thanking God for saving my husband's life two years and three months before his actual death. At that time, on April 22, 2000, Thomas left Providence Hospital in Washington, D.C. in the evening after seeing patients and was broadsided at a traffic light by two men being chased by police. His injuries were so severe that the emergency room physician at the Washington Hospital Center did not give him much hope of survival. The doctor told me that, rather than give me false hope about Thomas' recovery, he gave me a truthful assessment of his status but hoped for the best outcome.

Prayers went up immediately after my husband's accident. Patients, family members, churches, friends and acquaintances in other cities and states prayed for my husband. We later learned that a witness at the scene of the accident immediately prayed for him. I remember one of the physician's referred to my husband as the "miracle man" because he survived.

My husband did not resume his practice for several months. I became his nurse at home. Though he was used to taking care of others, I, my children and family members had to take care of him.

The time spent together during his recovery was truly a gift. We now had a lot of time to be together again. We took a Crown Ministry class to learn God's principles of managing money. He became more active working with the men in the church. We also attended a February couples' retreat prior to his July death. I thanked God for the couples' retreat because the retreat left me with the beautiful memory that we spent our last Valentine's weekend with Christian couples pledging our love to each other and learning how to use God's word to strengthen our marriage.

Criminal trials were held for the two men involved in the robbery and death of my husband. The trials were emotional and stressful and ended in two guilty verdicts.

I thanked God before, during and after the trials. He provided me and my children with friends and family who were by our sides during all the court proceedings. There were many others not physically present for the trials but supportive in other ways.

It seemed like the more I thanked God for his grace and mercy, the stronger I became. I continue to thank him daily. I don't take anything for granted, especially not life or the presence of my family. God has blessed me in so many ways. I have loving children, two dear granddaughters, family members, in-laws, friends, and a church family.

I continue to ask God to help me with my life and decision making. I still give him thanks. My faith is strong!

TRUSTING GOD IS THE ONLY WAY

By Rev. Joyce Gray-Thomas

Over the years I've learned to trust God in so many ways. He has blessed me in ways that are almost unimaginable. The Lord blessed me with three wonderful sons who I loved dearly and worked hard to raise and provide a good home for as a single parent. But my children became my whole life and now I realize, I was putting my children before God.

One day, I felt that something was missing in my life. I had no clear direction, even with the love of my sons. There was a loneliness that I couldn't explain. I remember one day when I was reading my mother's Bible and it so clearly said: *"Every knee shall bow and every tongue shall confess that Jesus Christ is Lord."* (Philippians 2:9-11 KJV) Eventually I re-dedicated my life to Christ and promised to trust Him and teach my children to trust Him.

Some years later, I felt God calling me into ministry, but I ignored Him because I *felt* I was not capable of doing what He was calling me to do. I would always ask the question, "Why Me Lord?" The *calling* constantly stayed on my heart. However, I was more interested in buying a home and preparing my family for a more comfortable life.

Then one day, one of my sons was killed in an accident at the age of 22. Afterwards, I became very withdrawn. I shut myself away from everyone and everything. I was angry with the world. I even refused to acknowledge God. I felt God had forsaken me. True to God's nature, He sent two Christian women from my church to visit me and provide comfort during my darkest hours. They prayed with me and shared God's Word. At first, I had no interest in listening to them talk about God, especially when he had just taken my son away, but these faithful women of God helped me to understand that we're all only here for a moment. They assured me that God loved me and that I was blessed to still have two living sons.

I now realize that God never left me; He just let me experience the outcome of making decisions on my own. I didn't have the wisdom then, before the tragedy, as I have now. The Scripture in Proverbs taught me a valuable lesson, *"Trust in the Lord with all thine heart; and lean not unto thine own understanding. In all thy ways acknowledge him, and he shall direct thy paths."* (Proverbs 3:5-6 KJV) Well, I now realize that I was trying to direct my own path and failed to trust and seek the guidance of God. What a big mistake!

In the days to follow, God turned my life completely around. It took time, but I slowly began to trust Him and to rely on the comfort and love I had for my other two sons. God's love and His light began to shine through my life. However, while going through the grief and pain of the loss of my child, I totally forgot that my living sons were mourning their brother in their own way. God touched my heart to help me realize that they also were suffering and needed their mother to help them through their sorrow.

It was then that I realized how much I needed God in my life. I prayed and asked God's forgiveness for not depending on Him in making decisions. Shortly thereafter, I received a deep inner peace that I had never known before and was no longer confused about my salvation or the love of God. Neither did I feel the loneliness I once felt in my life. I trust God and I now have a committed relationship with Jesus Christ. I am so thankful for His love and His Word that tells me, *"But they that wait upon the LORD shall renew their strength; they shall mount up with wings as eagles; they shall run, and not be weary; and they shall walk, and not faint."* (Isaiah 40:31 KJV)

In March 2009, I lost a second son to a street robbery, and three years later, on May 15, 2012, I lost my last son to cancer. This time I didn't shut myself away and blame God for all that had happened, because I know now that God did not give my children to me forever. He merely allowed me to enjoy a wonderful life with my sons while they lived. For that, I am truly thankful. I trust God's Word that says,

"For I am persuaded, that neither death, nor life, nor angels, nor principalities, nor powers, nor things present, nor things to come, Nor height, nor depth, nor any other creature, shall be able to separate us from the love of God, which is in Christ Jesus our Lord." (Romans 8:38-39 KJV) I never my lost my faith. I never lost my praise. I never lost my joy because I had learned to trust in Jesus.

So, to those of you who have lost children or a loved one, I know it's hard, but trust God; He will give you that peace that surpasses all understanding.

Shortly after the passing of my last son, I accepted God's calling into the ministry and the peace and joy I now feel is unexplainable.

THE GIFT OF LIFE

By Bridgette Ann Greer, Esq.

Life was pretty good prior to 1999. I was practicing law, had a decent job, owned my home, traveled and did what I enjoyed doing most — exercising. I jogged about 25 miles a week, lifted weights, and enjoyed water aerobics. I jokingly told my friends that my desire was to be on the front cover of *"Muscle and Fitness"* magazine. Around March of 1999, while jogging, I noticed that my breathing became more labor intensive. When I went to the doctor, he informed me that my reduced breathing capacity was caused by pulmonary sarcoidosis that created extensive irreversible scar tissue on my lungs. Ten years earlier, I was diagnosed with sarcoidosis in my eyes, which almost caused me to lose my vision. Despite my breathing challenges, I continued with life as usual and did not think as much about my health. Eight months later, in November, I was hospitalized for three weeks with pneumonia; that's when life began to change.

While hospitalized for pneumonia and sarcoidosis, the doctors noticed that mold and fungus were growing in my sputum samples. I had developed aspergillosis, which is an air borne disease. Undaunted, I continued life as normal after I was released from the hospital. By 2001, my pulmonologist said that in about five years I would need a lung transplant. I did not pay much attention to his diagnosis and just assumed that he was being overly precautious. Although I had to be hospitalized on many occasions for bronchial infections and had to use oxygen on exertion, for the most part, I just considered these instances as minor inconveniences to my already hectic schedule.

Over time, simple tasks became increasingly difficult to perform. I had a nagging hard constant cough that depleted my energy. When I drove to and from work, my co-workers would have to escort me to and from my car or follow me home. Once I arrived home, I would take a nap in my car (even in the winter) because I did not have the energy or strength to go into the house. Even with all this happening, I still did not think that I needed a lung transplant.

Fast forward to 2006, I had relocated to Durham, North Carolina in preparation for a double lung transplant at Duke University Medical Center (Duke). Duke was the only center that would accept me because other medical centers considered me "too high risk." I was in pretty good physical shape so undergoing the daily four hours of required physical therapy for transplant patients five days a week was quite easy.

Around 6 p.m. on March 13, 2006, while I was out eating dinner with my mom and my dear friend and church member, John Askew, Sr., I received a call from my transplant coordinator. She said it was time to head to the hospital because a compatible set of lungs had been found. For the first time since this journey began, I realized the gravity of what was about to happen — my life would be forever changed physically, mentally and spiritually.

Doctors anticipated the surgery to take six hours but when the surgeons attempted to remove the old lungs, they found aspergillosis had calcified and turned to bone. As a result, the surgery lasted 16 hours with a second team of surgeons called in. The doctors said that had I not been in good physical shape from exercising, I would not have been able to endure the surgery.

Oftentimes, I feel guilty knowing that on March 13, 2006, an 18-year-old man died and left me the opportunity to live. As my family and I rejoiced in having new life, there was a family somewhere that was grieving over the loss of life. This young man did not die so that I could live, *but*, because of his death, I have been able to live a very fulfilling and rewarding life. I do not know if it was the young man's decision or his family's decision, but someone made a very courageous decision to give the gift of life at an extremely difficult and painful time. And for that, I am forever indebted to the family as well as to God who directed them.

As I reflect on my life after the transplant, I think about the renowned surgeon at Duke who, in all of his experience and wisdom, told me that I would never make it out of surgery, and if I did, that I would not live longer than a year. In response, I told him, "You do not know my God."

I reflect on the friendships I developed with other transplant patients along this journey who have impacted and became a part of my life. I reflect on being a "member" of the "transplant club" — a membership that I never applied for or wished to be a part of. As members, we share similar experiences, fear, joy and hope for a brighter future; whose only desire is to live a healthy life and breathe freely. I reflect on those friends who are no longer here with us today. I reflect on God's faithfulness and that during my loneliest hours, He was always there beside me, comforting and strengthening me when no one else understood the solitude. Then, I reflect on the fact that I am here today not because I did anything right, or that I was the ideal patient. The **only** reason that I am here today *is because of God's loving mercy and His amazing, amazing grace.*

Life post-transplant consists of lots of medication, constant medical checkups and trying to remain free of germs and infections. Part of the side effects of being a transplant patient is the long-term detrimental use of anti-rejection medications. Although my lungs are faring well, and I have far exceeded the average life expectancy of medical statistics, the medication has taken a serious toll on my kidneys.

In November 2017, I was diagnosed with Stage 5 chronic renal failure and since March 2018, I have been undergoing peritoneal dialysis for eight-and-a-half hours nightly in preparation for a kidney transplant. When the time is right, I trust that God will provide a compatible donor, just like He did in the past.

As I look back over my transplant experience, I realize that my transplant journey had more to do with my spiritual growth and dependence on God and less about the many health challenges I faced. When I begin to fear the unknown, I look to God, the source of my strength and being...and then I know without a doubt, that everything is going to be all right.

SISTAS HOLD ON TIGHT TO THE ROPE

By Natashia Hagans

Sistas hold on tight to the rope...
You see this rope is a length of strong cord
made by twisting together strands of natural fibers...
While holding on to the rope sistas
our hands have interlocked with hard work, sweat, tears,
joyful memories, and visions of tomorrow...
So hold on tight with your dear life to the rope...

The first women to hold this rope was Eve
which might cause controversy...
Yes without a doubt Eve ate the apple
that bruised mankind...
But she birthed a nation of women who tried hard
with all their imperfections and conquered...
Yup Eve held on tight to the rope...

The next sista to hold on tight to the rope is Sarah...
Sarah wanted a child badly and at times grew weary...
But she never lost hope in God's promises...
By her obedience and faith she gave birth to a child...

Rahab the Harlot who betrayed her people
to help the Israelites...
The Samaritan woman at the well who had
an encounter with Jesus...
Mary the mother of Jesus who wept as her son was nailed
to the cross but rose three days later...
All of these sistas held on tight to the rope
leaving a powerful imprint for generations to come...

As time passed an abolitionist named Harriet Tubman
freed slaves successfully with the Underground Railroad...
Ms. Tubman definitely held on tight to the rope...
Rosa Parks who didn't give up her seat
to go to the back of the bus clinged to the rope...
The list gets deeper, Sojourner Truth, Coretta Scott King,
Mother Theresa, Helen Keller, Mary Bethune,
and Betty Shabazz...
Each held on tight to this rope a length of strong cord made
by twisting together strands of natural fibers...

Even in our present times sistas are holding on
tight to the rope...

Michelle Obama a lawyer and writer who beat the odds and
became the first African American "First Lady" ...
Michelle Obama coined the statement:
"When they go low, we go high"
This sista held the rope very high...

A young girl by the name of Malala Yousafzai
who survived being shot in the head to help females in her
country get an education...

Malala sacrificed a lot to hold on to the rope...
Right now as the world turns a woman named
Serena Williams who has been falsely accused of cheating
in Tennis and some want to boycott her legacy...
But with defiance and fearlessness Serena stated:
"I don't cheat to win, I'd rather lose"
Serena is holding on to the rope with dignity...
Can you hear that phrase with an echo "I don't cheat"?

So today in the present times with conviction: "Sistas hold
on tight to the rope" ...

This rope has history it is resistant, made with love,
golden, holds passion, endured, stained with blood,
and has paved the way...
Please sistas hold on tight to the rope...
Each ancestor that has held on to this rope has faced
sadness, depression, grace, strength, joy, peace,
anger and even rage...
But they survived and held on tight
to the interlocking woven fiber...

To every woman, millennial, generation x, y, z...
Make this rope so tight that as each person leaves an
imprint no one can see the gaps
because the rope is being held tightly...
Sistas hold on tight to the rope...
Carry on the legacy, the torch, don't let the fire dim...
The rope holds a future of blessings, strengths, mistakes,
golden opportunities, triumphs, setbacks, and
a sprinkle of sunshine...
So hold on tight to the rope my sistas it can bend
but never let it break ....
You see this rope is a length of strong cord
made by twisting together strands of natural fibers...

GOD'S FAITHFULNESS

By Deacon Shirley A. Harper

You never know how God is going to work. Whoever thought that on May 8, 2016, I would be in the hospital on Mother's Day?

Two days before, I had a doctor's appointment for a steroid injection for the carpal tunnel syndrome I suffered in my hands. After the injection, the nurse discovered that my pulse rate was lower than normal. Typically, the pulse rate is between 60 and 100 beats per minute (bpm), but mine was at 40 bpm. The doctor told me to monitor my pulse. Later that night, my pulse rate dropped to 30 bpm, so my husband called the nurse and he was instructed to take me to the hospital right away or call an ambulance.

My husband, Lawrence, took me straight to Holy Cross Hospital in Silver Spring, Maryland. Speeding down the highway, we were in constant prayer. I went straight to the emergency room. Although I never felt sick, only weak with no energy, I was dying and felt the presence of the Lord in that room. I looked around and saw defibrillator paddles to revive me in case my heart stopped beating. I know that this sounds strange, but I was not worried because I knew that the presence of the Lord was in that room. I could feel His presence and it was a very pleasant feeling.

Doctors rushed me into surgery, explaining that my electrical system that tells the heart when to pump was failing. A pacemaker was surgically implanted to help my heartbeat at a normal rate. Praise the Lord! Right after the surgery, I woke up feeling wonderful and very energetic.

I was 79 years old at that time and the Lord placed it on my heart to slow down, so I gave up some things I loved. One thing I reluctantly eliminated from my schedule was coordinating the Crown Financial Ministries with my husband. God had blessed us to coordinate that ministry for 22 years, and for that, I am grateful. We agreed to facilitate classes for as long as we could.

The Lord also laid it on my heart "to do all that I can, the best that I can, for as long as I can, while I can" for the Ministry of Jesus Christ. Only what I do for Christ will last. Today, I spend time texting encouraging, spirit-filled notes to my family in different areas of the United States. I pray that the Word will bring comfort as they receive God's help to live a faith-filled life.

It was easy to write this testimony because for years, I have written letters to the Lord every time I worried about something. I would use those letters to pour out everything in my heart that was concerning me. I didn't call a friend or even tell my husband about everything. I just talked to God on paper, starting with praise reports and ending with prayer requests. I continue to do this today. Afterwards, I always feel so much better. Sometimes I get answers that only the Lord could give me.

When I began to write this testimony, I just went back to my May 2016 notes to the Lord. Whenever I read back over my notes, I'm always amazed at the answered prayers and miracles that have happened over the years, especially this one.

WE SURVIVED!

By Alicia Hawkins

"I praise you, for I am fearfully and wonderfully made. Wonderful are your works; my soul knows it very well." (Psalm 139:14 ESV)

As I hear bombs explode around my home, I wonder if my family and I will survive to see another day. The house shakes from the bombs' impact, the windows rattle as if they could break at any time. With each boom, we close our eyes, knowing that a bright light will follow and illuminate the sky with all sorts of pretty colors. The bright red, evil light is one that we fear as a present, real and awful reminder that we live at war.

My story began in 1974 in San Salvador, El Salvador. My parents were teens when they fell in love in 1972. My mother, Alicia, was 16 years old when she birthed my sister who was stillborn. I came two years later, during the same week that my dad, Jose Luis, graduated from high school. We lived a beautiful simple life in my grandparent's shack made of straw and mud, with metal sheets for a roof, an outdoor wood stove and an outhouse. We grew coffee beans, vegetables and every kind of tropical fruit imaginable. Before the war, my cousins and I would play outside all day, climbing trees and building forts in the woods. We didn't have electricity or running water, but we were blessed and happy because of the love we shared, and because my grandfather built a well for us right before he died.

Selling water from the well didn't make us rich, but it brought us financial stability, the kind that allowed us to pay for very basic necessities to survive. With our family living off the land and growing most of our food, life was beautiful and simple. We attended school, family, and church gatherings. Our home was filled with the principle of working hard; more importantly, I was taught to always do the right thing for the right reasons, no matter what. My God, my faith and the character traits instilled in me prepared me for everything that was to come, so that I could survive!

In 1975, my baby brother was born. However, by 6 months old, he became ill and later died in my mother's arms while she was away at her mom's house. My mother had traveled by bus to her mother's home outside the city to get help in caring for my brother whose health was declining quickly. My dad had stayed in San Salvador to work. Because my parents were poor and could not afford a formal funeral home service, my mom decided to bring the dead baby home, so my father could say his goodbyes. The military had set up checkpoints along the bus route because there were rumblings of a civil war and that a militia group was organizing an uprising. My mom carried her dead baby during a daylong bus ride, passing him off as a sleeping baby through various checkpoints. Dad did get the opportunity to say goodbye.

A little over a year later, when I was 2 years old, my mother decided to leave my father and start anew. She took me to her mother's home and then joined a caravan traveling to America for a better and brighter future. My mother made a grueling trip all alone by bus from El Salvador to the United States. She had one small bag with a change of clothes, a blanket, water and some food.

My mother's bag, with my baby dress inside as a keepsake, was stolen during the cruel, dangerous journey. My mother's sisters Candace, Goldie, Naomi, Gretta and Glo said that I stopped eating, speaking and refused to walk in response to losing both my parents. But it was the love of God and the family's love that helped us all survive. After about a year, my father did locate me and sued for custody. However, authorities placed me, then 4 years old, in an orphanage while they conducted their own investigation. I remember about eight children surrounded my bed as I cried my heart out around these strangers. I also recall, they warmly and lovingly stroked me.

My father eventually got custody of me and remarried when I was 5 years old. He built us a home that had running water, electricity and refrigeration. He educated himself and eventually became an engineer and a professor at a local university. He worked hard and made certain I received a great education at a private Catholic school. Although life seemed good, happy, and normal with my new family, I still wondered what happened to my mother and why she didn't communicate with me.

In 1984, when I was 10 years old, my mind focused more on the war and whether our home would be bombed than clothes, shoes, music and other traditional teenage worries. I have clear and vivid memories of the war and saw things no child should ever have to witness. Thankfully, we survived and became strong in faith because of it.

When I was 14 years old, my mother finally got established, saved money and sent for me to relocate in the United States. To be honest, war life was normal in El Salvador and my future wasn't a concern to me. I had a great education and had planned to attend the Catholic University (UCA) in San Salvador. Still, to me coming to the United States was a dream come true. I could finally have the 'Mommy' that I had wondered and dreamed about. I yearned for her love and touch and couldn't wait to live the dream. However, after I arrived, the dream faded quickly. My mother was an undocumented immigrant, earning a minimum wage while working three jobs just to survive and to feed me. This was not the dream I had anticipated. I was now living in a brand-new country, in a new culture, and had to learn a new language. There were new people, and no known family or friends. Everything and everyone were new, including my mother. Life had been hard on my mother and her demeanor was not warm like Dad's; she seemed cold and unaffectionate. Life turned hard for me too. Since arriving in the United States in 1989, I discovered a heart issue that impacted my health. I survived sexual abuse and an abusive boyfriend. And, I survived a near-fatal car crash.

By the grace of God, I met my husband, Rick, in 1996. We became friends, got married, and built a beautiful life together with two beautiful, amazing, strong, God-fearing and God-loving children: Taylor, 16, and Ethan, 12.

In October 2013, at the age of 38, I was diagnosed with stage three or four breast cancer. I am a firm believer that God, prayer, and faith saved me. Since the diagnosis, I've had a double mastectomy, 1 ½ years of chemo, six months of radiation, heart surgery, multiple blood transfusions, a failing liver and kidneys, pneumonia, staph infection in my chest, and breast reconstruction. I am three years in remission and praising God for every single day and every single pain that I feel. I have asked God to please allow me to be here, on this earth, long enough to raise my children with my husband, and to help me see my mother live the happiest time of her life.

This testimony and my strength come from God and from my amazing, beautiful and strong mother, loving father and stepmother, in-laws, John and Carolyn, and a supportive and dependable husband. The number of blessings I have encountered along the way are too many to keep track of and count. Let's survive together by keeping God at the center of our lives and learning how to welcome and make the best of what is given to us.

BEING OBEDIENT REQUIRES A SERVANT'S HEART

By Inez Henderson

One of the most rewarding experiences I have had in my Christian walk has been serving as a caregiver. God first blessed me to care for others from 2008 to 2010 and then provided two other opportunities that overlapped, the first from around 2011 to 2013 with the last one beginning in 2011.

Initially, I was uncertain and concerned about my ability to take care of anyone, and asked myself, "do I want to do it?" My mother-in-law, Ma K as I called her, had been living in Detroit with her youngest daughter (my sister-in-law) for about 10 years. When my sister-in-law began asking for help to care for her mother from her eight siblings, those that responded lived in Maryland and California.

My husband Ronald is the oldest of the siblings. He felt a real responsibility to see that his mother was cared for. In one of Ronald's earlier conversations with his mother, he had promised her that she would not be put in a nursing home if she ever became ill. Though I was not aware of that promise until later, and knowing he was worried, I wanted to take some of the pressure off my husband. So, I encouraged him to invite her to live with us in Upper Marlboro, Maryland.

I had just retired from my job as a high school guidance counselor after 36 years in the Prince Georges' County Public School District. Our children, Carla, Kenra and Rahman, were grown and lived elsewhere. We had an empty nest, although I was looking forward to spending time with my four granddaughters and one grandson. Though this was a big change, I knew it was the right thing to do to open our home. Ma K and I had always gotten along well, and it was very important to me that I support my husband and yield to the promptings of the Holy Spirit. Once Ma K joined us in 2008, I enjoyed our time together. We would do little things like brushing and rolling up her hair at night and cooking holiday meals together. She was an excellent cook! I spent two of the most satisfying and enjoyable years with Ma K, until her death in 2010.

After the death of my father, Lonnie Thornton in 2001, my mother, Inez Thornton lived alone in our family home in Detroit. My oldest sister, Hazel, and younger sister, Lonetta, helped Mom manage the four-bedroom house while also living in a separate residence. When that setup no longer worked, they sold the family house and my mom moved to an assisted-living apartment. We noticed early signs of dementia however and were told that for her safety and wellbeing she needed 24-hour care. After much prayer and many discussions, we decided to purchase property that would include a place for Mom.

Hazel sold her house and we pooled our resources together and prayed. Although it seemed to take forever, God showed up and showed out! My sisters were able to find a duplex that allowed each person to have her own space while Mom lived on the lower level with Hazel. Though I had retired, my sisters still worked at this time, so they hired caretakers to assist my mother during the day. My contribution was to provide respite for them as much as possible.

Before Ma K moved to Maryland, I visited Detroit every month or two to help with Mom. Now that I did not have that responsibility, I would take a week at a time and assume all the responsibilities for my mom's care in Detroit, including cooking, cleaning, washing or whatever else needed to be done. This became an extra special time for me because, not only did I get to spend time with my mother, but also with my sisters.

While working together to meet Mom's needs, my sisters and I would talk and laugh about some of the things she would do. We would reminisce about the past and catch up with what was going on with relatives and friends. It was an excellent time for sharing and bonding. It was simply wonderful being there and giving them a respite.

My third opportunity was caring for my mother's youngest sister, which began around 2011 and ended with her recent death in October 2018. "Auntie" as we affectionately called Aunt Hazel, relocated to Maryland after her husband died in 1993. At 75 years old, Aunt Hazel sold a house in Jamaica, New York, found a house in Maryland and purchased it. She then packed up everything to be brought to Maryland and arranged for a driver to bring her and her two pets to her new Maryland home. Until her 90th birthday in 2011, she was totally independent.

Ronald and I noticed changes in Aunt Hazel's thinking and memory. She began asking for help with bills and other responsibilities she previously had been able to handle on her own. Auntie begin to talk with me about how she wanted her personal property to be handled. She hired a lawyer who wrote her will and declaration, establishing me as her power of attorney. She talked me through what she wanted to be done regarding her funeral and burial. She went over her insurance policy and other important papers with me as we completed her business while she still could reason and make decisions. Eventually, she moved into a community assisted-living facility, which provided excellent care for years.

God has been faithful every step of the way and in every challenge that we have faced. As Aunt Hazel showed more signs of dementia, she became verbally abusive and combative. Often, I wanted to let it all go but God's strength, guidance and direction kept me where He wanted me to be. Ronald had a special relationship with her and often could talk to her and settle her down. It was a wonderful feeling to be able to take care of things as she had specified and to be able to reflect on the wonderful life God had blessed her to live, and myself to be a part of it.

What God showed me through these similar but different experiences was that I needed to learn how to truly give of myself; my time, talents, possessions, treasures and, any other gifts He had blessed me to possess. When I first retired, all I thought of was sleeping in, having no schedule, and coming and going as I pleased – with no demands or restrictions. I was torn and uncertain how caretaking would change my life. Because of my decision to be obedient, God blessed me with an overwhelming sense of satisfaction, fulfillment and joy. What I learned, as a result of all this, was that I could move out of my "comfort zone" and take on something new and different. I knew these choices were the right ones to make and I felt God's approval and the assurance of His presence. Each decision reinforced my commitment to being "a servant." I praise and thank God for giving me the privilege of having these opportunities and the strength to be obedient.

ON THE ROAD, BUT NOT ALONE

By Aravia L. Holloman

My first job after earning a master's degree from Pennsylvania State University was with Gulf Oil Corp. in Pittsburgh, Pennsylvania. I was hired as a systems analyst, a good position that paid well but was located 405 miles from my hometown of Ivor, Virginia, a tiny, rural town in Southampton County. I knew absolutely no one in Pittsburgh so I traveled home alone as often as possible for four years.

My favorite time to start my 8-hour trip home was around 2 a.m. I even packed my car at night, just before leaving. The Pennsylvania Turnpike, the route I drove, is a curvy, twisty piece of highway. At times a few tractor trailers and I were the only ones on the road. Not once did I experience any car trouble or negative encounters, other than inclement weather.

God was truly with me on each trip. I never gave a thought that traveling alone for such long distances, during early hours was not the best thing for a black female. All I knew was that I wanted to go home, and God saw that I made it safely every time. God did not give me a spirit of fear, but one that is unafraid. He is my protector.

RECOGNIZING JESUS

By Tanya E. Hood

I was 2 years old when I lived with my Grandmother Williamae and my dog, a St. Bernard named Tonda, in Northeast
Washington, D.C. I thought Tonda was a horse and rode on
his back all the time. He was my best friend. Grandmother
was known as the "Candy Lady" because she sold candy to
neighborhood children who came to our house. Candy-filled
jars stood on a board she laid across the hallway radiator
near the front door. One day, deciding I deserved a piece of
the candy, I mounted Tonda and moved toward the board
to grab a candy jar. I was not close enough nor steady as
I reached for the jar, pulling down several candy jars, the
board, me and my "horse."

The crash sound and dog yelp alerted Grandmother Williamae and she rushed from the kitchen with a look of terror in her eyes - a look I had never seen. Usually, a smile
on Grandmother's beautiful, caramel-mocha colored face

would light up the world. Eyeglasses made her beautiful brown eyes extra-large and you could see the love radiating from within her. This day, I saw terror. I saw it in her approach. I saw it in her yell; and, I saw terror as she raised her hands.

As my agitated grandmother approached me, Tonda rushed toward her and I darted into the living room, a forbidden area. The living room was off limits. Plastic-covered furniture, a china cabinet full of decorative dishes no one ever ate on and a fireplace fit into the room that no one ever seemed to enter. A picture of a black velvet Jesus, complete with a blue background surrounding this brown-skinned, black-haired figure, hung on the wall next to the fireplace. The other walls held photographs of family members. On a glass coffee table centered in the room was a photo album.

Did you know that a glass coffee table's height and a toddler running for dear life into a room she's forbidden to enter are bound to collide? I didn't know as I ran face first into the glass coffee table. All I remember is the picture of the black velvet Jesus. I was told that at the pace I ran toward the table, the force from the impact should have blinded me from bone fragments that would have entered my skull. The deep gash between my eyes is a physical reminder of that moment. It was also the moment I recognized Jesus.

From that day on, I recognized religious symbols every-where. I noticed the cross on my grandmother's neck and the mezuzah, a scroll with biblical passages on one side and a name of God on the other, by the doorframe on our house. I was aware of pictures of Jesus at other people's houses too.

Reflecting, I became aware that you can know Jesus at an early age, as I did at 2 years old. The religious symbols were constant reminders of His existence. When people asked about my scar, Grandmother Williamae used it to introduce them to Jesus.

THERE'S NOBODY LIKE JESUS

By Denise Branch Jackson

One early Saturday morning in July 2010, I got a telephone call from my mom who was crying and said she was bleeding. I sat straight up in bed, knowing this was serious. My mom, Jeanette, was about to celebrate her 71st birthday. She lived in Washington, D.C. and called me in Springdale, Maryland, because she needed a ride to Kaiser Permanente and didn't want my brother George, and sister Sherry to know. I am the oldest daughter so it would fall on me to be her first call. I didn't know how bad this could be, but she apparently did.

Before retiring, my mom worked more than 30 years at Holy Cross Hospital, in Silver Spring, Maryland, in the operating unit. Then, a position was created for her at a new Kaiser Ambulatory Center in Kensington because doctors she worked with at Holy Cross had requested her at Kaiser. She was the only certified registered technician in this area. Her position: Certified Registered Sterile Processing and Central Service Technician.

At Kaiser that morning in 2010, my mom was examined and given an appointment with an oncology specialist who ran some tests and told us it could be cancer. Weeks later at the next appointment, the oncologist said that the test results found that my mom had stage four bladder cancer. OH MY GOD!! My world started spinning out of control. "Not my momma! This can't be true; we're going to prove this doctor wrong!!" I declared. Then, we cried so hard, trying to wash the cancer away with our tears. "This just couldn't be happening!" I said. "She had retired less than two years before, only to face this!! Nope, not happening!! We got to have a plan!"

Then the journey with my mom began. An eight-hour surgery at INOVA Fairfax Hospital in Virginia removed the cancerous bladder. Working for the federal government, I knew my leave would not be enough to care for my mom. So, I went to my supervisor and senior officer to request an indefinite telework schedule. I became my mom's main caregiver because my brother and sister's jobs would prevent them from being at every appointment or treatment for my mother. But, my sister, brother, Uncle Eddie and Aunt Carolyn and I became a caregiving team.

We slept at her house on Eastern Avenue in Northeast Washington, D.C. in rotation, accompanied her to the hospital and stayed in the rehab rooms with her. We learned her medication and dosage schedule to help manage the pain. Her schedules and care were our lives. My mother's only sister, Aunt Lois, kept her spirits up with daily phone calls. And my cousin, her son Anthony, kept Mom in touch with family news and activities. And in two years of caring and fiercely protecting my mother, we came to really know that woman. We always saw her as brave but now we saw her fear and her faith.

I understood faith because I was baptized at age 16 at Mount Calvary Baptist Church on Emmett Drive in Alexandria, Virginia. I later joined First Baptist Church of Highland Park in Landover, Maryland around 1994. I was an active church member, developed a circle of Christian friends and worked for more than 25 years as a youth leader in the Awana Ministry. But I was fearful that my mother's relationship with the Lord wasn't deep enough. I focused my prayers on her salvation. The Lord blessed both me and my mom with an amazing home health aide, Ms. Florence, who took my mother's relationship with the Lord to a new level. I know that I will be forever grateful for that gift from the Lord.

My mom had a special bag put in place of her bladder, so we had to learn how to drain it properly. It was inside of her like a bladder, so drainage was delicate and somewhat complicated. We didn't really know how complicated until the first time it wouldn't drain. We had to take her to the Kaiser emergency center, the first of many late-night drives or day trips to the center that had the professional personnel to quickly resolve most problems. All my life my mom was a fighter. Anything that involved her children she supported, pushed us out of our comfort zone, exposed us to different cultures and the arts. Now, we were fighting for her and with her.

Life continued for me. Even with so much going on, I still had to work most days by laptop or going into the office. And my work was falling behind. When I was in the office, I worked well after 9 p.m., trying to clear my backlog to improve my statistics. The work security staff eventually got used to seeing me running through the halls to exit the locked building after 10 or 11 p.m.

The treatment plan that my mother's doctors had put in place at the start of this journey worked until about June 2012. My mom had seen her last three granddaughters, Reshe', Imani and Brittany graduate from high school and had taken a family cruise in celebration. She also enjoyed seeing her only grandson graduate from college. Now, the treatments were no longer showing positive results and Kaiser placed her under the In-Home care program. She would no longer see her doctors. With that change, my mom's anxiety increased, and her condition started to deteriorate. So, by December 2012, she had her peace.

I returned to work a few weeks later but it took a few months to really feel back in sync with the work. I found myself under pressure by upper management who wanted to know why my work wasn't caught up and my statistics not improved. When things did not improve on the job, pressure continued and adverse action was imminent, I didn't know what to do but pray. I prayed to the Lord to help me! I kept on praying because I was too stressed to do anything else. Then, the Lord did an amazing thing! He moved upper management to tell my supervisor that I should seek counseling through our employee assistance program. I didn't know that if I sought help from an onsite therapist, I would be protected from any adverse action!

The therapist helped me through mourning the loss of my mother and taught me how to manage my stress and anxiety levels. I was able to reduce my workload and improve my statistics. And guess what else the Lord did for me? I had been praying for a promotion before my mom got sick. I didn't pray that prayer anymore because too much time and opportunity had passed. One day recently I had to update a policy that required an updated salary report. I hadn't checked my salary in years. Well, when I went into the employee system to get my current salary, the Lord had provided the promotion in salary without the stress of a new position. Halleluiah!!

The LORD said, *"Sit in the place of honor at my right hand until I humble your enemies, making them a footstool under your feet."* (Psalm 110:1)

A BLESSED MIRACLE AND SURVIVOR

By Rev. Nicole S. Jalloh

I am a miracle and I'm alive to tell it. I have seen the Lord do miracles over and over again, both in my life and in the lives of my family members.

In January 2006, I was a victim of domestic violence. I was living in Oxon Hill, Maryland with my then 20-year-old daughter and 8-year-old son when a stalker entered my residence and shot me. The bullet entered my right temple, ricocheted back toward my right ear and exited right above my lip. I was conscious the entire time. My daughter and a friend ran in as the shooter left the scene. She dialed 911 as I lay on the floor in a pool of blood. As I lay there I prayed, *"Lord, Jesus Christ, please let me live to see my son grow up. Save me, save me, don't let me die."*

I had a relationship with the Lord at the time. At 34 years old, I was an active member of a Baptist church in Washington, D.C. I sang in the choir, attended Sunday School, and worked with the children's church, Awanas, and Women's Ministry.

Moments after the shooting, an ambulance came and rushed me to Prince George's Community Hospital's Trauma Center where I was treated for two days. Initially, the doctors wanted to give me a blood transfusion, because I had lost so much blood, but I prayed to Jesus and cried out so I would not need one. Jesus answered my prayer because I did not have to get a blood transfusion. Hallelujah and thank you, Jesus.

During my long recuperation, I learned that God is a healer and that no matter the situation, He will work things out. I learned and grew to appreciate that God will bring us through all situations, no matter what they are.

The shooter served a brief time in jail and was placed under house arrest. However, he eventually got off because he hired a high-price attorney. Despite that, I still knew my prayer was answered. A year after the shooting, I delivered my second daughter, who is now 11 years old. The Lord let me live to see my son celebrate his 20th birthday in October 2018.

THANK YOU, JESUS!!! HALLELUJAH, HALLELUJAH, HALLELUJAH!!! I stood on the Lord's promises in Psalm 46:1 (KJV), "God is our refuge and strength, a very present help in trouble." Another key Scripture is Psalm 61:3 (KJV), "For thou hast been a shelter for me, and a strong tower from the enemy."

During that ordeal, I knew that my entire family was praying for me – those here in the Maryland area and in North and South Carolina. My message to family members has been to get their lives together and accept Jesus Christ. I realize we can be here today and gone the same day. Life is just like that. Stay prayed up and covered by the blood of Jesus Christ.

MY NAME IS VICTORY

By Beverly R. Johnson

My name is Victory. Y'all may know me as *Beverly*,
but *My. Name. Is. Victory.*
God spoke that *into me* even as I sat *on my mother's knee.*
Grace, peace, love, *glory.*
My. Name. Is. Victory.

I could stand here and tell you a story of sorrow and *pain.*
Of despair and lack instead of *gain.*
I could tell you about living in fear and without *hope*;
Or feeling like you're drowning with not even a *rope* –
to pull you in.

I could twist your heart *strings*
Describing terrible *things...*
And abuses... and *mistakes.*
Or of family deserting me, friends ROBBING me,
of men harming me,
And of folks out to *take, take, take.*

I could tell you about the lonely child
hoping to catch some love
With her eager *smiles*.
Or of the child turned teenager left to fend for *herself,*
Or how without guidance in the early adult years
She squandered her *wealth*.
Or of the soul-ties created through aimless *wiles*.
Or of the hardships faced going through so many other *trials*.

But I won't. Why? My name is Victory!!!

I WILL tell you of God's goodness and *grace*.
Of HIS love that saved me and slowed down my *pace*.
Of HIS mercy, so SWEET to save me time and *again*.
Of HIS magnificence that He still calls me his *friend*.

I will tell you of the INDESCRIBABLE joy
that SPRINGS up in my *soul*.
Of the happiness that keeps my jokes on a *roll*.
Of the UNSURMOUNTABLE peace that blankets me now
in every *situation* -
And the blessings that keep coming
like a well-needed *vacation* – from Life!

I want to impress upon you the REALNESS
of my relationship with my God,
My Abba (father), my instructor, my way-maker, provider,
redeemer, my *HEART*.

I have come to yearn for HIM daily –
Hating when we, no I, break *a part*... from HIM.

I stand amazed at what I have come to know about my
God... your God... our God.
I stand in awe of how he has revealed himself to me.
I stand in humility as I step into HIS presence.
I stand in "Thanks!!", OH GOD, that you would see me,
Inconsistent me, immature me, disobedient me,
As worthy of your *consideration*.
And within you I am made clean
and brand new by *consecration*.

You give me wisdom un-paralleled.
You grant me favor un-*matched*.
You provide me opportunities un-imaginable.
And you promote me from wayyy in the *back!*

You give me the VICTORY!!
Time and again
I thank you and praise you for being my friend.
I thank you and praise you for being born again.
And I accept my new name you've assigned me –

My. Name. Is. Victory.

COME BEFORE HIS PRESENCE WITH SINGING

By Brittany C. Johnson

"Make a joyful noise unto the LORD, all ye lands. Serve the LORD with gladness: come before his presence with singing." (Psalm 100: 1-2 KJV)

I remember it as if it were yesterday.

My first day back at school was only for half of the day. Being sick had not been fun. Neither was being out of school for more than a month, maybe six weeks. At that point, I was not sure. All I knew was "I'm tired of the needles and all the medical tests." There had been talk about disease and my heart. At 6 years old and in the first grade, I had so many questions. It was all too much!

Let me back up a bit. About six weeks earlier, my health had been fine. I was a normal kid, living in Augusta, Georgia and attending Dearing Elementary School in a nearby town. I was taking tests at school because everyone was saying, "First grade isn't difficult enough for Brittany. She needs a challenge." School officials were considering third-grade lessons for me. Maybe they were right; first grade was very easy. School was fun, although I did have to take weekly allergy shots. Everything seemed normal, with nothing to worry about. I even joined church and was baptized in kindergarten. Then things changed.

I'd been sweating a ton, even though I was freezing cold. My mother told the doctors about the sweating during one of my regular allergy appointments. When the doctor examined me, he found I had an extremely high fever. Off to the hospital Mom and I went. I thought I would be back at home that night. Instead, I was taken to a room and put in a bathtub of ice. I didn't understand why the hospital people would do that.

As days passed, Mom and Dad seemed to worry as any parents would. But my parents had a strong, close relationship with the Lord and worked in the music ministry. In fact, today my father is a pastor. At that time, they sang a lot of songs from church. My pastor, Rev. Frederick Favors, came by the hospital to pray. And get this, Grandpa even prayed out loud. I'd never heard that before. My family and friends surrounded me, always singing and praying. It was like they brought church service to the hospital.

After some time, the doctors figured out why I had the high fever, cold sweats, and hallucinations. I had a disease called Kawasaki syndrome, sometimes called mucocutaneous lymph node syndrome because it also affects lymph nodes, skin, and the mucous membranes inside the mouth, nose and throat. It was uncommon and gave me a heart aneurysm that made my heart's arteries become larger than normal. It was then that I understood why they sang and prayed so much.

After the diagnosis, I was in and out of the hospital for tests and treatments. The doctors monitored my condition throughout this period. My family and I talked about everything that was happening to me. I had always loved music and Mom had always talked with me about worshipping God, even when things didn't seem that great. I decided it was my turn to do what my family had been doing. I sang lots of songs as I went through days of tests, treatments, and healing. I talked with God a great deal too. I eventually got better and went back to school starting with half days, then full days as I became stronger. Before long, I was back to doing what normal 6-year-old children do and finished first grade.

Years have passed since those memorable weeks in first grade. Today, I'm healthy, full of life, and yes, I still sing. I have my own personal relationship with the Lord. My passion is helping others express themselves through the performing arts, especially singing. As an adult, songs of worship strengthen my faith and remind me that God's got me. The song lyrics remind me of the peace, love, joy, and healing that only our Savior can bring. God-inspired music will always be a testament to my faith. *SELAH*

MY JOURNEY THROUGH A TSUNAMI OF LIFE

By Dawn N. Johnson

We've all encountered storms throughout our journey in life. For me, that storm was devastating and took on a Tsunami effect, and life was no longer as I once knew it. During this storm, I lost myself and my purpose. My heart and spirit were broken, and I was shattered into pieces. I did not know how to bounce back or even if I could.

As I began to search for ways to put my life back together, storms continued to come. Every time I felt like I had enough strength to move forward, something else happened. It wasn't until I fully relinquished myself to Christ did the storm begin to shift, allowing some light to shine in on my situation.

A close girlfriend, Rocky, invited me to a women's conference at her church. The theme that year was becoming "Unstoppable." I was desperate and yearning for a lifeline, so I attended the three-day conference at First Baptist Church of Glenarden and began to experience Christ in a manner I never experienced before. It was as if every message was being spoken directly to me.

The first night during praise and worship, I received the Holy Ghost. I began to sing, cry, and praise God for his goodness. My life began to change at that moment as I realized just how amazing Christ is and how much He loved me. I began to look at my life differently. I was able to shed the tears I needed to shed during the first wave of my storm. In that moment, I realized I had everything in me to be an unstoppable woman in Christ. The conference sparked an interest and desire for me to seek Christ further. As a result, I joined the discipleship course at my church, the First Baptist Church of Highland Park.

The weeks leading up to discipleship class, I was both apprehensive and excited. When class began, it was great with facilitators who gave us material to study at home. The first book we studied was "Growing Strong in God's Family." I believe I did just that. I learned the importance of study time. I started memorizing Bible verses and fellowshipping with classmates. I attended almost every class; some would say my attendance was stellar. The week leading up to the last class of book one, I became ill. I went to the hospital where

I later found that I was having a thyroid crisis, also called a thyroid storm. I was learning about Christ and growing strong in His family, and well, my faith and strength were being put to the test. My mother, Dawn, and family were worried and concerned. Oh, but God! I prayed about my health and let it go. I applied the needed treatment and improved. During this storm, I experienced the power of faith.

The second book, "Deepening Your Roots in God's Family," was great. But life continued to happen. Class was good and becoming more intense and more intimate. As a result, I began to set aside some alone time with God. During this class, my faith and prayer life grew stronger and I became closer to Christ. I started praying, reading, fasting, and studying more. During book two, my mom became ill. She suffered a stroke in front of me and my daughter, Destiny. This was devastating for the two of us to witness.

My daughter and I followed the paramedics to the hospital in our car. On the way, she asked, "Mom, what are we going to do?"

I asked, "What do you mean Destiny? We are going to follow Grandma to the hospital."

She said, "No, Mom, what are we going to do without Grandma?"

My heart stopped, and tears began to flow. I took a deep breath and said, "We pray, Destiny."

After praying, a sense of peace and calmness filled the car and our tears were gone. When we arrived at the hospital, my mom was alert, talking and most of the symptoms that I saw at the house were no longer visible. During this storm, I experienced the power of prayer, healing and deliverance.

"Bearing fruit in God's Family," the last book of the program, was amazing. A few days before classes began on book three, I received a call from my Aunt Gale informing me that my dad, Carl Johnson, was being taken to a hospital. I left work that evening and headed to the hospital. When I arrived, I was escorted to the family waiting area where other members were gathered. When the door opened, I saw disappointment in the eyes of my uncles, hurt and devastation in my daughter's eyes and disbelief in my sister Denaysha's eyes.

She looked at me and simply said, "He didn't make it; he's gone."

At that moment, I felt like I had a choice to either breakdown in the family room or outside the room. I walked out of the waiting room and proceeded to the other side of the hospital. I think I lost every piece of dignity that evening. By the time I made it out the door, my legs buckled, and it literally felt like someone had ripped my heart out of my chest and I wept. My sister came behind me and told me to get it together. She said I could not cry in the waiting area in front of the people who were there with sick patients. I stood up and fell into my baby sister's arms and she held me. I got myself together and went to pay final respects to my dad.

I could only imagine how grief would overtake me when I entered his room. But, to my amazement, God intervened as He always does. When I entered the room and saw my dad, I simply said three words: "Thank you, Jesus." I said it repeatedly. I began to thank Christ for the life my father lived and the legacy he left behind. That day I experienced strength, thanksgiving and gratefulness.

Dad was a jokester, a family man who loved immensely. He was a man who endured, like many of us, life struggles. He overcame life's difficulties by finding Christ and persevered. His life depicted a picture of what true discipleship looked like in his every day journey and how God shaped, rebuilt and customized him for his glory.

The grief that I suffered during my dad's death was a journey that I never envisioned. This journey was built on disbelief, as I had just seen my dad, and even prepared dinner for him prior to him suffering a massive heart attack. Through that devastation of heartbreak and pain, I developed a level of strength and faith that I did not know were obtainable. Faith and prayer had become a daily dose of medicine that I incorporated to help me get through the day. I am grateful that

God called him home during the highest peak of his journey. God allows our setbacks to be those things that position us to be able to bounce back through his love, grace and mercy.

I've always known about Christ. I knew what He was capable of. I knew Him as a provider, healer, deliverer, and a way maker. But now through my journey, I know about Him because of the personal experience and the intimacy that Christ and I now share. I fell in love with Christ and it's my desire to encourage others to do the same. Without going through some of the toughest storms, having a great support system and attending discipleship class, I would not have discovered my spiritual endurance. I would not have known how much faith I had or that I could persevere from the Tsunami that touched down on my life. I am confident now that God will never put more on me than I can bear.

MOMENT OF TRANSITION

By Kayla Johnson

I knew something was wrong. As I awoke to the sight of my father and mother pacing up and down the dark upstairs hallway by my room and debating whether to wake up me and my sister, they used such graphic words as "deceased," "expired," and "suicide." I recall this life-changing event like it happened yesterday. It's still clear as a summer day. At 5:30 a.m. on January 6, 2013, as the dim pink shade illuminated my room from the sun beaming off my blinds, my mother said, "Joel is no longer with us." That came after she said in a gloomy tone, "Remember, no matter what happens, God is in charge."

My body went numb. My heart shattered like a glass thrown to the ground. Everything was in slow motion and I felt as if I was in a never-ending maze. I didn't know where I was. Everything looked grey as my mind started spinning in circles, trapped without a way out. My head was throbbing like the heartbeat of a newborn baby. It felt like a nightmare, "Nightmare on Elm Street" and Freddy Krueger was chasing me. I was scared. Scared that I lost one of my closest friends. I can still remember falling on my knees as a young child and cousin Joel, who we affectionately called "Smook," being there to pick me up and tell me, "Wipe those tears sister! You're too tough to cry." That was always his role to protect and comfort me like a big brother.

His death was a suicide and doctors speculate that the cause was depression. The unfortunate thing about suicide is you never know when it's going to happen and who's thinking about it. My cousin was one who spoke his mind and told everyone how he felt. He was a comedian in my eyes; he always kept me laughing. I can remember the endless times we would run around the house, jumping off couches, throwing chairs, and just having the time of our lives.

As soon as my uncle, his father, would come home, we would stop and act as if we were doing homework the whole time. I also remember the time my aunt threatened to kick all of us out of the house for being so loud while she studied for an exam. We were three rowdy kids running around a house as big as a mansion, uncontrollably knocking things down, falling over and tossing ourselves. We would make so much endless noise that the neighbors would knock on the door telling us to keep it down. Joel was more than a cousin, he was my best friend.

It's scary how someone can suffer from depression — a common and serious medical illness that negatively affects how you feel, the way you think and how you act — and not show it one bit. I would have never thought in a million years that my 'Joyful Joel' would be depressed at age 19. He never showed symptoms of being depressed, his smile would brighten up my day, and his hugs were always warm and fuzzy. But the facts were, my cousin suffered from depression from the age of 12 and it was undisclosed to the family.

I grew up with Joel. We attended the same schools, church, family events and spent countless hours with each other. We learned from each other and built an unbreakable bond and valuable relationship. Not only did this incident affect me mentally, but physically and spiritually. My thoughts were scattered, my eating habits were off, and I could not remain focused. After his death, I began to question my relationship with God. If God was always with my family, why would I experience something so detrimental in my life?

Throughout the grieving process, many life lessons were learned. Soon after Joel's death, my strength and tenacity to live became obvious. His death taught me to cherish my loved ones and that God will put us through trials and tribulations to force us to grow closer to Him. This experience has taught me, regardless of life difficulties and conditions, life is always worth living. God placed me on this earth to change lives, bring healing to others, to learn from past experiences, and accomplish goals.

Finally, no matter the obstacle, I have learned to be persistent and endure to the end. This incident has taught me that life offers new opportunities, even during negative circumstances. I am now more passionate, focused and determined to earn my Bachelor of Science in Nursing so I can continue to be instrumental in bringing about healing. This situation has motivated me to achieve my goals. I now embrace life, and I will not give up on the many opportunities that await me.

SURVIVOR OF DOMESTIC VIOLENCE

By Shirley Johnson

As a child, I attended church services and Sunday School every week at Newfield Baptist Church in Washington, D.C. I joined the church and was baptized at 11 years old. I was the secretary of the Sunday School for several years. Also, Grandmother Webster, who lived with my parents, me and my four siblings, would have Bible study in our home during the week.

In 1964, my cousin introduced me to Lawrence, a young man who was nice and listened to me when I spoke. We became friends, and after a year, we moved in together. Things were going well; I had a daughter in 1965 and a son in 1968. But Lawrence started to change. Whenever he drank alcohol, he would become jealous and possessive. If a male showed any attention to me, we would argue about that when we got home. After a while, he would start arguments in front of his family or friends at his mother's home, at a cabaret, or when a visitor was in our home. He was a nice person during the week, interacting with me and the children, but on the weekend, he would get drunk and then turn vicious.

Eventually, the arguments upgraded to slaps and punches to my face. I missed work frequently because of black eyes, bruises and, one time he cut me on my ankle. I was out of work for about two weeks. When these fights started at home, a neighbor or I would call the police. When he cut me, I filed charges and the police put him in jail for the weekend. These altercations occurred only on the weekend when he drank alcohol. He was fine if he did not drink. I needed him financially because I was working for a temporary employment agency.

I was constantly praying and asking God, "How can I get out of this relationship?" I left him after he cut me, and I was able to get an apartment in Glenarden, Maryland with the assistance of my parents and one of his sisters. My younger sister moved in with me and we shared the costs. Also, I got a job as a receiving clerk at Hechingers on nearby Brightseat Road when the store first opened. Not only could I walk to work but after 60 days, I was promoted to receiving supervisor.

Lawrence continuously tried to get me to take him back and to see his five children by this time, but I stood firm. His family members were calling and giving me updates on how he was doing. It felt so good to be able to go to work and attend church on Sunday. Even the children were more at ease and happy. They did not have to listen to the verbal abuse and watch him physically abuse me. After six months, however, my sister married and moved out. I started letting Lawrence come to see his children and we talked about our problems and getting back together.

Eventually, we started living together again because he was working steadily and wasn't drinking. Things were going well, but he started to change again. He seemed to be angry all the time and had started to drink again. He lost his job because he was drunk when he went to work. This caused us to be evicted. So, we moved to Coral Hills, Maryland. This meant I had to catch the bus to get to work. Thankfully, I was able to get a ride with someone I worked with who lived nearby.

On a Friday in 1975, I met Lawrence at the Giant Food store in Coral Hills. He was drunk and started saying, "I'm going to kill you." I ignored what he was saying and continued to shop. I went to the checkout counter and we caught a cab home because we did not have a car. While riding home, he kept repeating, "I am going to kill you," all the way home. After arriving home, the children helped put away groceries and I fixed dinner for us.

After dinner, I decided to leave the house because I was scared of him. He had never threatened to kill me before. He continued to drink and say he was going to kill me. I really thought he was going to kill me. I asked him what was wrong and what did I do to upset him. He did not respond. The kids did not hear him say those words.

I informed the children, whose ages at that time were 8, 11, 12, 13 and 14, that I was going to my girlfriend Betty's house and gave them her phone number, if they needed me. I called and checked on them and they were fine and said he was sleep. I spent the night at Betty's and called the house the next morning. Lawrence said he was sorry, and the children wanted to know if I would prepare spaghetti for dinner. He sounded like he was sober and I decided to go home. I asked my girlfriend's sister, Ruby, to take me home.

When I arrived home, the children were so excited to see me and asked was I still going to make spaghetti for them for dinner. I started cutting up the onions, garlic and green peppers. He came up behind me and started shaking and grabbing me, which made me turn to face him. His facial expression was distorted, and he started saying, "I am going to kill you" and he continued to shake and punch me. To stop the abuse, I stabbed him, not realizing I still had a knife in my hand until he collapsed to the floor. The children came out of their bedrooms asking what happened. They started to cry as I called the Emergency Medical Technicians (EMT).

When I heard the sirens coming down the street, I went to the front door and looked out. They pulled up and parked, but they did not enter my home until the police arrived. I felt like I was in a fog and I started to pray that he was going to be all right.

The police asked me what happened, and I told them. He was pronounced dead at the scene. I told my oldest son to call my mother and sister and let them know what happened. The police handcuffed me and took me to the Forestville Police Precinct for questioning. I remembered my children crying for me and asking where I was going. I was scared, wondering what was going to happen to my children and me. I knew I was going to jail for a long time.

When I arrived at the precinct, the police placed me in a room and handcuffed me to the floor. The room was painted green, had one window, table and two chairs. I continued to pray for my children and me. The longer I stayed in that room, it felt like it was going to close in on me. Police allowed me to leave the room only to go to the restroom. While I was praying, I heard my sister speaking loudly to the detectives, asking them to check the official records that detail numerous reports of domestic violence.

Eventually, they released me and told me to inform them if I left town. There were so many people praying with and for me. God is so awesome!!!!! There was no inquest or trial or jail time. It was like the paperwork was lost or it never happened. Of course, I know that it happened. God has always been there for me and I know He continues to be with me. This happened more than 40 years ago when resources for domestic abuse were scarce. There were no hotlines, shelters or homes for victims of domestic violence. Now, there are all types of places to stay, financial assistance, Hope Groups and even police help. I know that God has forgiven me for Lawrence's death, but it is still heavy on my heart. Taking a person's life is not a good thing. I committed a sin. The Bible says, *"Thou shalt not kill."* But 1 John 1:9 (KJV) says, *"If we confess our sins, He is faithful and just to forgive us our sins, and to cleanse us from all unrighteousness."*

Today, I am living a Christian life, enjoying retirement and my family.

GOD IS BIGGER THAN DISCRIMINATION

By Femi Kay

Starting in kindergarten my mom had me in church. She would either take me or send me along with her tithe in a small white envelope. She was a great role model, praying on her knees through her 60s. It was my mother who shared "with Christ I can do all things but fail." Although my faith wasn't as deep then as it is now, I realize that God was preparing me for unexpected challenges that caused unbelievable hurt and pain. Not only am I an African American who was subjected during that time to blatant discrimination and racism on the job, but I was a "big-boned black female," proud of my heritage and culture. I was extensively targeted by blacks and whites, alike.

While attending Bowie State University and Howard University in my early 20s, I began working with federal government agencies as part of Cooperative Education. This program provides the opportunity for the student, educational institution, and a federal department or agency to enhance a student's career through a combination of classroom studies and on-the-job training. The goal is for the student to serve the nation while gaining experience for future employment opportunities. Once I was hired full-time as an accountant and auditor, I traveled extensively and had a wide variety of experiences. But discrimination also was rampant.

I worked for five federal agencies during my 10 years of employment. A couple of the federal agencies hired me in Washington, D.C., but relocated me to such states as Florida, Texas, and California. During this time, I filed four informal and formal Equal Employment Opportunity (EEO) complaints with the federal government. But what my bosses meant for evil, God obviously meant for good. Why? I won all four complaints and over the last 29 years, God has blessed me with more than $1 million from the cases. I thank God that I stood on His Word and He knew, I only did my job. Despite being treated unfairly, I was hired by other agencies and earned promotions.

"Let us not become weary in doing good, for at the proper time we will reap a harvest if we do not give up."
(Galatians 6:9 NIV)

The tactics used by my federal bosses were vicious. At one point, they moved my office to the so-called "dungeon," which was the basement where surplus equipment, dusty desks, old calculators and other out-of-date materials were kept. At other times, I would leave an open Bible on my desk and prayed daily.

"The name of the Lord is a strong tower; the righteous run to it and are safe." (Proverbs 18:10 NIV)

Discriminating supervisors hated it and would slam their office doors after passing by my cubicle. Some co-workers were told not to befriend me, but they did so anyway and acted as witnesses to help me win my EEO complaints.

"The Lord is my helper; I will not be afraid. What can man do to me?" (Hebrews 13:6 HCSB)

During an Employee Relations Luncheon for one agency, an official described me as their "token black." Another job illegally fired me and had to reinstate me. God eliminated one of the discriminating agencies.

"For I know the thoughts that I think toward you, says the Lord, thoughts of peace and not of evil, to give you a future and a hope." (Jeremiah 29:11 NKJV)

With the $1 million in settlements God provided, I was able to stay home and raise my two sons, one of whom was sick from infancy until age 3. God healed him and sustained our needs, as we stayed committed to our tithes.

"And my God shall supply all your need according to His riches in glory by Christ Jesus." (Philippians 4:19 NKJV)

Reflecting, I now understand that God blessed other people through my hardship. I assisted two other black women with Federal EEOC cases, as well as one woman with a discrimination suit against a private company. I started a program called EGAS – Everybody Got A Suit. The settlements forced some policy changes and, I am certain, made some bosses think twice before engaging in discriminatory practices. At another time, I learned that when officials investigated my case, they discovered that others had been mistreated as well and returned pay and allowed promotions to them as well.

"Carry each other's burdens, and in this way you will fulfill the law of Christ." (Galatians 6:2 NIV)

I encourage other women to stand up for their rights. Just as God led me to the right people who taught me to read carefully rules, regulations and contracts, He will do the same for others. I also learned to "document" everything. I knew I was right. I was standing on the truth. I was doing my job. My final advice: Trust God when all others forsake you.

*"But blessed are those who trust in the Lord
and have made the Lord their hope and confidence.
They are like trees planted along a riverbank,
with roots that reach deep into the water.
Such trees are not bothered by the heat
or worried by long months of drought.
Their leaves stay green,
and they never stop producing fruit."*

~ Jeremiah 17:7-8

Chapter Three

Contributors L through R

"But blessed are those who trust in the Lord and have made the Lord their hope and confidence."

~ Jeremiah 17:7

THE STRATEGIC MOVE OF GOD

By Vernell Lawson

To God be the Glory.

Four days before Labor Day, on August 29, 2018, I was on vacation in Belize, Central America. My grandson, Zachary, and I were in the pool when I lost my balance and quickly slipped from 5 feet of water into a rushing 8 feet. I panicked but God had my 12-year-old grandson there to pull me to safety.

If he were not strategically placed there by God to help me through that split second, I dare say I would not be writing this testimony. To God be to glory for all the good things He has done for me!!!!

SOMEBODY PRAYED FOR ME

By Rev. Dr. Patricia H. Love

Today, as I look back over my life, I can certainly give God all the glory, the honor, and the praise. He has been good to me down through the years. He has brought me a mighty long way, from birth to beyond the scriptural promise in Psalm 90:10 of 70 years. When I was a child, being obedient was not an option; children were expected to do what they were told, that was the bottom line. I have carried that same mind-set to my Christian life and my relationship with God through Jesus Christ. To obey God's commandments is my heart's desire.

I was born in Bucksport, South Carolina and lived with my parents, Albery and Wilhelmina Hunt, and 12 siblings. While my parents did not necessarily reward us for being well behaved, I knew my parents loved me and I did not want to stir up their wrath by disobeying them. My mama took us to church, but as I grew into my early teens, I attended church alone and became active. I served as Sunday School secretary, sang in the choir, participated in and assisted with planning church events, programs, church conventions, and choir parades.

As I attended church, I soon began to understand that going to church was more than coming to a building. My knowledge of God and His Son, Jesus Christ, led me to understand what "salvation" meant. I learned I could choose life by surrendering to Jesus Christ or choose death by surrendering to Satan, in other words, heaven or hell. Thank God, I chose Christ. It happened on a Thursday night on September 12, 1963, during a revival at our church, the Salem African Methodist Episcopal Church.

At that time, churches would have people who had not claimed an allegiance to Christ to sit on the so-called "mourners' bench" in a certain section of the building. I went to the mourners' bench, repented of my sins and confessed my belief and trust in Jesus Christ for my salvation. Praise the Lord! My father and I were baptized on the same Sunday in the Waccamaw River. Glory be to God! What a change has come over me, and I know that my relationship with Jesus has gotten sweeter day by day on this Christian journey. He has brought me safe this far.

As I grew, I did not always know what I was doing or what I was supposed to do. I understood that God always had His eye on me, just as He watches over the sparrow. He kept me when I did not know He was keeping me. Who wouldn't serve a God like Jesus Christ? He truly is ALL we need. Glory, hallelujah to His holy name!

So, I journeyed through life with Jesus carrying and keeping me. I graduated from Whittemore High School, moved to New York a month later and four years later, married Leroy Phillips. Leroy was in the U.S. Army. We moved to Kreuzberg Karserne, Germany, and lived there three years until his reassignment to the United States, at Fort Riley, Kansas. I moved back to Bucksport to deliver my first child, Xavier, in August 1972. Shortly afterwards, my husband moved the family to Washington, D.C., where my second child, Yolanda, was born in August 1974. She is the heart of this testimony.

Yolanda was two weeks old when I visited my sister Costella, at the Greater Washington Hospital in Washington, D.C., where she was scheduled for a procedure. At her bedside, I began hemorrhaging. Hospital officials put me on a gurney and as I lay there, I thought I would surely bleed to death. But God! I had to have an emergency operation; however, the doctors could not stop the bleeding with this procedure. The doctors came from the operating room and told my husband, I needed to have a more intense operation to stop the bleeding and that my life was in jeopardy without this operation. My husband had to make a life or death decision for me, and he did. He gave his consent for the operation to be done. God was watching over me just as He always does. Praise the Lord!

Somebody prayed for me. My sister, Costella, was a praying woman and I know she was praying for me. My sister would not let the doctor perform her procedure until she knew that I was safe. While my sister was praying, my mama and brother Jonathan were on their way from South Carolina to the District of Columbia. By the grace of God, they arrived safely. Although I was barely able to make sense of anything, I saw my family standing around my bed.

My brother said, "Sis come on now, you have to pull through, because you have a beautiful little girl and a son who need you." That's all it took, a reminder that I had someone who needed me, and I could not give up. By God's grace, and with the prayers, doctors gave me six units of blood, and I stayed 10 days in the hospital, followed by two weeks at home without lifting or holding my baby girl. It was only the grace of God that healed and strengthened me to a healthy life again. My Jesus had the final say in the matter. Thank you, Jesus!

But God! Yes, I'm still here to testify of His goodness, mercy, and grace. Nobody, but God! I remember and have learned that when you need a doctor in an emergency, Jesus will be there on time. I had an issue of blood, and by His stripes, He healed me. Today, I am 71 and He keeps me. He brought me through this, and He brought me through that, with my husband and our children and He is still lighting my way. Even when I don't understand, He makes a way. Only God can do these things in Jesus' name. AMEN.

He is the Healer. He did it for me and He will do it for you, even if it is someone else praying for you; the prayers of the righteous availeth much. Trust God and remember it's all done in His timing. He knows about all urgencies, and He is still in the prayer answering, miracle working business. Seek His face, keep praying until something happens. He said in His Word, *"Call unto me and I will answer thee, and show thee great and mighty things, which thou knowest not."* (Jeremiah 33:3 KJV)

Lord God, I am humbly grateful to You for being my Lord and Savior, and for your one and only Son, Jesus Christ, and for this opportunity to be a witness of your goodness to me. Keep us all in your care. AMEN!!!

IF YOU DON'T DO ANYTHING ELSE FOR ME, YOU'VE DONE ENOUGH

By Dorothy Marks-Fontenot

How can I say thanks for the things you've done for me, are lyrics from the song, "To God Be the Glory." I have, as we all, many things to thank God for. I would just like to highlight two special miracles that occurred in our family.

My husband Al and I have a blended family. When we married in 2006, Al brought to this blissful match two daughters, Kimberly Bookman and Michelle Parker; a son, Albert Fontenot III, and their families. I brought to the match, two daughters, Courtney Anne Baker, who is married with three daughters, and Lillian Regina Marks, my oldest. We affectionately call our new family "the Brady Bunch."

The blended family worked better than I thought, although I hadn't thought much about it. Albert and I both grew up on the west side of Chicago. His mother was my Sunday School teacher and his dad was the assistant pastor at Lawndale Christian Church, located a block from my family's house. My parents, Paul and Arie Mae Turner, attended Metropolitan Missionary Baptist Church with its spirited shouting and noisy services that frightened me.

I was too young to understand that the people at Metropolitan were simply praising the Lord. I was baptized at Metropolitan at the age of 10. When I understood better what the shouting meant, it didn't frighten me as much. When I later started to attend my parents' church, I played the organ for Sunday School in the morning and the piano for Baptist Training Union in the afternoon, as well as sung in the Junior Choir.

Eventually, Albert married my girlfriend, Beverly, and I married Hubert Marks in 1970. I became a widow after 26 years of marriage in 1996, while Albert's wife died a few years later in 2003. We reconnected a few years later.

The first special miracle came in 2014 when Albert and I lived in Long Beach, California, and our daughter Michelle, who lived in St. Louis, Missouri, was diagnosed with cancer and required months of chemotherapy. Her entire family was afraid – her two sons, Josiah and Jaylen Hickman and her new husband, Kenneth Parker; and, his son, Denver.

Of course, Albert and I were praying, and fortunately, Michelle remained positive. Her brother and sister-in-law and children took up residence at the hospital. Several of her nephews shaved their heads to support her hair loss. At the time, I couldn't help her much because I had developed stomach problems. I was sick daily and unable to eat, although I had no appetite anyway. I lost 20 pounds.

The doctors apparently thought my symptoms were simply caused by stress from worry over Michelle. I have since had my gallbladder removed, which has corrected the problem. I still must take medication daily, but I feel much better now. Maybe, there's a miracle there too. God made it possible for me to heal so I could later still provide some support to Michelle. However, God answered our prayers because presently, Michelle is cancer free and her family has grown closer.

The second miracle involves Regina, my single daughter living in Atlanta, Georgia, who battles the side effects of diabetes. Regina was planning a trip to Florida with her sister Courtney and family. Courtney is a Registered Nurse Practitioner, and a few days before she arrived in Atlanta, Regina began to have vision problems. Regina thought she only needed her contact lens' prescription changed to correct the problem. She had just told me she she was so proud of her 20-pound weight loss. I am a retired RN and should have been concerned with the classic symptoms of uncontrolled diabetes that Regina was exhibiting. My daughter finally went to Urgent Care and found her blood sugar was over 700 — normal blood sugar usually is around 100. Regina had driven at night during the rain to Urgent Care in an unfamiliar area. Although her vision was affected by the high sugar level and the inclement weather, she made it to the facility without an accident.

She didn't pass out. Praise God! She spent the night in Urgent Care, and called her sister and cousin in Texas, but not me. The next day she called me when she got home. The fact that Courtney came to Atlanta within hours gave me comfort and saved me a plane trip. That was God's grace! Courtney's family stayed with Regina an extra day, went on to Orlando, Florida and stopped by on their way home to see how she was doing and whether she was following doctor's orders. She wasn't.

Regina was depressed and angry. "Why me?" she said she asked God, which is typically what people feel when faced with a life changing diagnosis such as diabetes. Her sister was able to help her with her depression, her diet and the change in her lifestyle. Regina's name is forever in our prayer vessel at First Baptist Church of Highland Park in Landover, Maryland. I tell her continually, "if God doesn't do anything else for you, He's done enough."

Truly, we are thankful. God has been good to the Fontenots.

DOWN THROUGH THE YEARS, GOD HAS KEPT ME

By Susan A. McLaughlin

I was born in 1941 into a family of sharecroppers in Chatham, Virginia. I did not realize how poor my family of four sisters, five brothers and parents were at the time because the Lord provided all that my family needed – food, shelter, work and love. I started school at 6 years old, attending a one-room building where children were taught up to the eighth grade. I continued my education in Chatham through high school. I even completed one year at St. Paul's College in Lawrenceville, Virginia. However, my faith was tested when I moved to Washington, D.C., because I left a tight-knit community where church was the center of life and found myself in a totally different environment. I worked different jobs until I got married in 1964. Shortly thereafter, I started working for the FBI, a job I kept until I retired in 2003. YES, GOD KEPT ME!

My husband, Thomas, and I have two girls and one boy. We believe that education is very important, so we used our resources to send two of our children to local private schools and one to a boarding school in Massachusetts. Each child has earned both undergraduate and graduate degrees. YES, GOD MADE A WAY!

In 1986, I was diagnosed with cancer. I went to the doctor thinking I had a tumor; I had no idea it was breast cancer. I had a lumpectomy and five weeks of radiation treatments. Defying the odds, I recovered within six weeks. God had prepared me for this time because I had built up enough leave on my job to financially cover me. When I worked, I did not take sick leave unless I was sick. So, when I had the surgery and needed recuperation time, I did not miss a paycheck during the entire six weeks. It was all God! I didn't have to worry about finances. YES, GOD KEPT ME!

Twenty years later in 2017, I was dealt another shocking diagnosis. It was breast cancer again! This time, I decided to have a mastectomy. After surgery, I received four rounds of chemotherapy that really made me sick. I was so thankful for the help my husband and children provided. I also received an outpouring of support from my nieces, nephews, and church members. I lost my taste buds with the medication I took, and I constantly ached all over. There were days I felt like I couldn't make it. I kept telling myself, "you got to have faith, God is going to bring you out." My problem was that I would feel great just before the next treatment and then feel bad again afterwards. It was like a roller coaster; today feeling real, real good then get chemo and the next day feeling like crap. It's a mental game going through cancer, you have got to think "He is going to bring me out. God is going to bring me out." You must keep that in your mind. If not, you won't make it. I did not lose faith. YES, GOD KEPT ME!

I believe that God felt my pain and heard my prayers. I was overwhelmed during my illness, exhausted and worried about how I would overcome breast cancer again. I prayed for God's healing and He answered me. He told me that he would get me through this season. He told me, "I will fix what is broken, rest in Me." AGAIN, GOD KEPT ME!

I believe I have healing energy. Often, I close my eyes and visualize myself full of life. I meditate on God. I know if I don't ask, I won't get, so I ask. God's healing energy is in every part of my being. I am immersed in a healing, purifying light. If there is an area of special need, I focus my attention on it. I know Gods' healing energy works in that particular place. JUST KEEP THE FAITH!

I have learned to let go of any concerns and trust the divine activity within that heals and keeps me well and whole. I relax and let God's healing light renew my mind and body.

I know that Jesus is the only one who can do anything and everything. In God's loving care, I am charged with new life. YES, I AM IN GOD'S CARE!

"Then shall thy light break forth as the morning, and thine health shall spring forth speedily: and thy righteousness shall go before thee; the glory of the LORD shall be thy reward." (Isaiah 58:8 KJV)

LIVING A BLESSED LIFE

By Theresa M.T. Melton, a.k.a. "TERECKA"

My prayer is that my testimony will encourage and uplift others as it continues to strengthen me in my journey and my ministry of comedy.

I spend a lot of time caring for my parents, Eugene and Corrine Thomas, who I love dearly. When my mother was diagnosed with Stage 4 kidney failure in 2011, my life's journey took a detour that landed me at the official start of a comedy career. My mother and our family were devastated after receiving the kidney diagnosis. But I could not allow her to be defeated. She has always been a woman of faith and a woman of God.

The only thing I could think of telling my mother at that moment was, "Mom, at least you are not pregnant." Although my joke did not change her diagnosis, it did provide her some comic relief and comfort of knowing that I was not going to allow her to cry her way through her illness. She is a fighter and I was determined that we were going to focus on getting her well but enjoying the journey through laughter, spending time together, and entertaining each other as much as possible.

What I did not see coming was God placing me in front of audiences and making others laugh at me, with me and with themselves. In 2008, I entertained more than 300 women at a First Baptist Church of Highland Park Women's Retreat. The Rev. Dr. Minnie Washington, co-pastor of St. Timothy's Christian Baptist Church in Baltimore, Maryland, had witnessed me tearing into the room and igniting the women with laughter and excitement. All the while our First Lady, Weptanomah Davis, tried to videotape my performance to prove to Pastor Henry P. Davis, III, that she was not making it all up. Even I had to admit I was off the chain that night.

Being the keynote speaker for that evening, the first thing out of Rev. Washington's mouth when it was her time to speak was "I am going to give you a stage name. I anoint you "TERECKA." I don't think Rev. Dr. Minnie, or the Highland Park ladies, had ever experienced the wrath of my comedy, hence the well-chosen name for wrecking the audience with good, Christian fun and entertainment.

I did not welcome the name at first. When people would call me by the name at church, I would say, "That's not my name." But it had become my name. Rev. Dr. Minnie anointed me with the gift of "TERECKA." After much prayer about it, I realized it was all a part of God's plan to take me to the next level, where He wanted me to be...growing in my ministry of comedy.

Once I accepted this blessing and realized this is who I am, doors began opening for me all over. In 2015, I graduated from the DC Improv Comedy School. I have performed at the DC Improv, the National Council of Negro Women, Inc. Annual Scholarship Awards Luncheon, and numerous corporate and private events.

Today, years after my official start in comedy, I would not have imagined that I think of jokes all day long. Even as I drive into work in the morning, I call my mom while she is on dialysis three days a week to tell her how much I love her and to share my latest jokes. She looks forward to laughing and encourages me to make others laugh too, even when the jokes are about her, my dad, my husband Julius A. Melton, or one of my many dysfunctional family members. I remind them that since I am entertaining them for free, the jokes are going to be extra "hot and on fire" because I am talking about them. Family is the best comedic material.

I truly love the journey God is leading me on through my ministry in comedy. Even when people are serious, a little down and out or not so confident in themselves, laughter changes their outlook. I have embraced it and now I see God's blessing upon my life through the spirit of laughter and the ministry of comedy. And, I am so blessed to have my husband of 27 years, my parents and my extended family and friends take this journey with me. They have been extremely supportive, encouraging and great material as I laugh and make others laugh along the way. And, I dedicate this testimony to our Cocker Spaniel of 15 years, Raider, who left us in May 2018.

If I had to do it all over again, I would not change one thing. This is indeed part of my comedy *herstory* but know this: "TERECKA" lives on. There is still so much more of my story to tell and I am blessed and grateful there will always be something to laugh about.

PRAY WITHOUT CEASING!

By Elizabeth Newburn

"I will bless the Lord at all times: his praise shall continually be in my mouth." (Psalm 34:1 KJV)

The day I started work in the Diagnostic Center at Providence Hospital in Washington, D.C., I had a strong relationship with Christ. That love affair started years earlier when I worked as a surgery technician or operating room nurse at both Doctor's and Children's hospitals in the nation's capital. You see, I had been through some stuff. I was raised a Catholic, where they taught that we could only pray to God through priests or saints. We did not study the Bible because Catholic church officials said everything we needed to know could be found in the catechism. All that teaching came into question when my mother was diagnosed with cancer. We felt helpless, relying on priests who could only say that my mother's condition was tied to her "lack of faith." She died.

Shortly after my mother's death, I was diagnosed with diabetes. I hated to even breathe my health was so poor. As my condition worsened, I was afraid to pray to God myself because of those Catholic teachings. But one night, I was suffering so much that I ventured a "mustard seed prayer," just in case the Lord could hear my plea: *"... verily I say unto you, If ye have faith as a grain of mustard seed, ye shall say unto this mountain, Remove hence to yonder place; and it shall remove; and nothing shall be impossible unto you."* (Matthew 17:20 KJV)

He heard my prayer!! When I went to the doctor and the phlebotomist drew blood, my sugar level had dropped. The doctor asked, "What did you do?" I started to cry and confess that I had prayed to God. The doctor assured me he was not angry but surprised with the improvement. But I was confused and scared; I went to confession to divulge my attempt at prayer. I was really messed up.

I knew absolutely nothing about the Bible and had a lot of questions. One day while I was on my way to Mass, I heard on the radio a message from Frederick KC Price of the Crenshaw Christian Center in Los Angeles, California. Fred Price said that we don't have to pay the price for our sins because of the atoning work of Jesus Christ, God's son. Shortly after that, a friend of mine invited me to her Baptist church for Bible study that was taught by the associate minister.

After only a few lessons, the minister met privately with me to learn more about my background. I told him about my good-paying job at Children's Hospital and how I was the mother of twins. I opened up to the associate minister because I had viewed him as I viewed the priests in the Catholic Church. Next thing I knew, I was pulled into a meeting with the church pastor who said that God had told the associate minister I should be his wife. I did not like that man but was told by the pastor that if I did not marry the associate minister, I would be telling God I did not trust Him. I was scared.

I was in my 30s when I married the associate minister. His knowledge of the Bible was the only thing that attracted me to him. He was possessive, not allowing me to talk with folk or have friends, and he moved us to Gaithersburg, Maryland to break ties with family and friends. Then, my daughter was born. My husband eventually became abusive. He even drove me to and from work each day to maintain control. When I approached the pastor about the behavior of the associate minister, he told me to be "long suffering."

When the twins were 5 years old, I discovered the Christian Life Center, a Pentecostal church attended by a coworker. It was here that I learned about prayer. On Sunday afternoons, I would convince my husband that the twins and I needed to go for a ride, or I would make up other excuses to leave the house. We were fascinated by the church services where members were running, leaping, shouting, falling to the floor and speaking in tongues. The drawbacks, of course, were that they did not believe in watching television, wearing makeup, cutting or dying your hair, or wearing shorts. That didn't matter to me at that time. It was a praying church and that was what I needed. After that first visit, the pastor said, "Welcome home." I cried.

The Christian Life Center had three prayer rooms: one was sparsely furnished to accommodate those who wanted to walk around and pray. Another room was equipped so you could sit or kneel in prayer. The third room was empty to allow those who wanted to lay out before the Lord and pray could do so. I had a vision during one of my prayer sessions that confirmed my salvation. Another time while meditating in the prayer room, someone touched my shoulder and I heard a voice say, "Peace I give unto you, and my peace shall set you free."

That divine encounter led to a dream later that night that provided my life Scripture of Psalm 34 and assurance of an escape from my abusive marriage. I later joined Refreshing Springs Church of God in Christ, a place that nurtured and grew my children. Also, before my children were off to college at Florida A&M University in Tallahassee, Florida and the University of Pittsburgh in Pennsylvania, the church recognized my stellar parenting skills with an award. My baby daughter was in high school at that time.

While working at Children's Hospital, I started a ritual where I would arrive early each day and walk throughout the corridors and pray over the workspaces, the equipment and for my co-workers. That would come after I had enjoyed the quietness of the mornings and prayed as I drove to the hospital. Not a day would go by without me starting the day this way.

When I transferred to Providence Hospital, not so much for a promotion but to hide from my soon-to-be ex-husband, the prayer ritual continued. When I moved to admittance and registration at Providence, I prayed this way too. I tried to consult God about what I should do and how I should do it. I enjoyed my work at the hospital and my colleagues. Best of all I treasured then, and more so now, my deepening relationship with God and his Son, Jesus.

It was prayer that led me to my current church, First Baptist Church of Highland Park in Landover. I continue to grow in Christ.

WAITING ON MY MIRACLE

By Wanda Leigh Offley

I was living in Washington, D.C. on Hamlin Street, Northwest when I suffered a stroke on January 9, 2017. I was babysitting my grandsons and granddaughter when it happened. I knew I was having a stroke because I recognized the symptoms: numbness and weakness in my arms, face, and legs on one side of my body; and, my speech started to slur. God gave me enough strength to contact my high school friend Sharon who called 911 for an ambulance to come for me. God also gave me strength to walk out of my house and get into the ambulance. Sharon came to stay with my grandchildren.

I spent one month in the National Rehabilitation Center at the Washington Hospital Center. I suffered a second stroke that left me unable to swallow, talk and eat at the Arcola Rehabilitation Center in Silver Spring, Maryland. I was transferred to Holy Cross Hospital in Silver Spring, then back to Washington, D.C. to Georgetown University Hospital, where I was fed from a feeding tube for 10 months. I lost 100 pounds as I learned to eat healthier foods. God taught me patience during this time. I learned how to be patient with God and let Him work out my healing in His own time.

I reached the maximum recovery in rehabilitation at the Heartland Health Care Center in Hyattsville, Maryland. I've been at Heartland for two years and can eat and talk again. My next step is further rehabilitation. God has truly blessed me and returned to me the abilities I had lost to the stroke.

My blessings are expected because I've known the Lord as my personal Savior since 1985. On that day 34 years ago, my son James, then 11-years-old, and I were baptized together at the First Baptist Church on Randolph Street, Northwest in Washington, D.C. That experience changed my life; I had been separated from my husband six months and was headed for a divorce. When I found the strength to accept Christ; He helped me through a tough period in my life. As my relationship deepened, I became more active at church, singing in the choir, managing a Boy Scout Troop and the Day Care. I joined First Baptist Church of Highland Park on Christian experience on Saturday, October 6, 2018.

I am still unable to walk but I know God will bless me with the ability to walk again one day. I know He will because God is able to do "exceedingly and abundantly above anything" I could ever think or imagine. I believe in Him wholeheartedly, and I am expecting and waiting on my miracle because God is able!!

God is my Savior and the fortress in my life that keeps me going through my bad times. I love the Lord with all my heart and soul! Nothing can separate me from the love of God!!!

FROM BROKENNESS TO WHOLENESS:
How God Can Heal A Broken Heart

By Kathryn P. Osborne

"What becomes of the brokenhearted who had love that's now departed" are words to a popular Jimmy Ruffin ballad that had many teenagers and young adults of the 1960s swing'n, sway'n and sing'n to the Motown Records' Soul Label tune. Back then, I never dreamed or imagined I'd be singing this song 30 years later, as an adult woman with a broken, shattered heart after experiencing my first 'real' love and a relationship that could have led to marriage. My hope and spirit were both shaken.

I had not long graduated from Prince George's Community College in Largo, Maryland when I began working at a test preparation center in Northwest, Washington, D.C. During this time, I met a Nigerian doctor who had come to the center to prepare for his licensing exam. We hit it off and started dating, although the bulk of his time was spent studying. I was serious about the relationship, but he wasn't. I thought of marriage, but his goal was to take his exams and move on. I honestly thought our relationship was going somewhere.

I had accepted Jesus Christ as my Lord and Savior, at this point, and worked in the church. When things started to fall apart with the guy, I viewed myself as a woman covered by God's grace as I struggled through choices, challenges and the ups and downs of life. Nothing ever prepared me for the dark season that tested my faith and forced me to question my relationship with God.

Nothing ever prepared me for the weeks and months I cried myself to sleep, only to wake up at the break of day and put on makeup to cover the tears. Nothing ever prepared me to drive to work each day with tears, flowing from my eyes like rain, rolling down my cheeks. Tear-stained hands fixed my face before walking into the workplace one more time, seeing him face-to-face; the one who broke my heart into a million pieces.

Days turned into weeks, weeks into months and then a year. Because I was grounded in the Word and truly believed in God and His Son Jesus, I decided it was time to heal. The tears I first cried from night to day, over my broken heart, now flowed as I cried out to God and asked

Him for healing. I began to realize that only God can fix a broken heart and that I needed a closer relationship with Him. I rededicated myself to Him.

The Holy Spirit revealed that "I am the Lord that healeth thee." When I opened my heart, and received His comfort, I knew I was set on the path from brokenness to wholeness. This journey may be traveled by many women. I am now free, and you can be too. This experience and process allowed me to draw closer to God and again give Him my heart. I believe, know, and boldly proclaim, that surgery can be performed on a weak and damaged heart; but a broken heart must heal. I am now living with a new heart and renewed spirit.

Sister friends, when we are faced with many challenges and struggles in our lives that are emotional, spiritual and physical, we must stay strong and resilient on the journey from brokenness to wholeness. On this inspirational journey, we are required to be quiet. So often when challenges come, we go through life, running, trying to fix things ourselves and listening to a lot of different voices.

But we must go to God and listen to what He has to say. The journey also will require you to be still. Rather than moving and asking for advice from family and friends, I believe that God will have you sit down and study his Word. This will draw you to Him. And, the journey will require you to be close. Trust in God. As you are quiet, still, and close, God will speak in that soft and gentle whisper. You will know that it is He who speaks.

"...But the Lord was not in the wind: and after the wind an earthquake; but the LORD was not in the earthquake: And after the earthquake a fire; but the LORD was not in the fire: and after the fire a still small voice." (1 Kings 19:11c -12 KJV)

YOU HAVE NOT BACKSLIDDEN TOO FAR FROM THE LOVE OF GOD:
Come Back Home

By Taneya Pair

I remember like it was yesterday, I joined church in April 2011. I was sitting in the back on the left side of the old sanctuary of First Baptist Church of Highland Park in Landover, Maryland. I felt a need for something, though I wasn't quite sure what was in store for me. As I made the move to join, it was like I was breaking free into a space that was foreign and unknown to me. I was 23 years old and engaged to be married. That's another testimony for another time.

Two weeks after my baptism, I stopped attending church. Two absent Sundays turned into two years. I returned to life as I knew it; I remained empty, lost and confused. I knew that I wanted my life to be different but there was a tug that just wouldn't let go. I returned to clubbing, fighting, drinking and everything else. The streets were holding me;

destroying my life. The Sunday that I returned to church was in January 2014. My decision to leave church was never because of any thing anyone did to me. I was so damaged as a young woman that I was ashamed and thought that God wouldn't want to love me. I was raised without my dad, so I did not experience love from a father; I believed that I would not experience love from anyone during my lifetime. That included love from God too.

However, the day I rejoined church and re-dedicated my life to Christ, Pastor Henry P. Davis, III spoke of backsliders. I wept and took the long, powerful walk towards the altar. I knew enough was enough. I wanted to experience the love of God and walk into a new life. My fear growing up without my dad, was if my dad couldn't love me why would I think this Supreme God would want to love me? I was so broken, but I forced myself to believe that God wanted to love me. Yes, I was scared and nervous because I felt so low about being loved by God. I would always think to myself, "who do you think you are?"

I wasn't raised in the church and was upset with my mom because I felt that I missed out on so much from my life. I would always think, "Where is my foundation?" What I didn't know was that God was establishing and forming His foundation uniquely for me from His hand. The woman of God that God birthed, was not inherited, programmed, mentored or coached by man. I had only God to lean on, so I did.

My life is a testimony of God's unfailing love and protection. I came to God broken, hurt, lost, unsettled and all that I was; God received and took me into His home, into His arms and kept me. God loves the backslider, just as He does anyone who has slipped away but now has come back home.

NOTHING BUT
THE GRACE OF GOD

By Laverne A. Parks

Often tears run down my cheeks. There is nothing wrong with me; in fact, it is quite the opposite. My tears flow in gratitude for God's goodness, grace and mercy toward me. There were times I was embarrassed by this; that is no longer the case. I know God does not make mistakes; this is who He made me to be. My tears are not because of timidity or sadness. The Bible says, *"For the Spirit God gave us does not make us timid, but gives us power, love and self-discipline. So do not be ashamed of the testimony about our Lord or of me his prisoner. Rather, join with me in suffering for the gospel, by the power of God."* (2 Timothy 1:7-8 NIV)

My tears of gratitude are because God breathed the breath of life into my body for another day. I am grateful for Raymond and Thelma Baylor, my loving, devoted parents. I am blessed to have loving and caring people in my life. I have family, extended family, neighbors of 30 years, church family; and sometimes, just the kindness of strangers bring joy to my life. My children, Kimberly, Arlene and Raymond bring me joy, although they are sometimes challenging. My niece Tammy, whom I consider to be my first baby; a son-in-law, Norris; a daughter-in-law, Rasheda – they are all true blessings. I have 10 grandchildren, plus a nephew who is like a grandchild. Their ages range from 9-year-old twins (our miracle babies) to a 31-year-old. I have four great-grandchildren, who all have been a blessing in my life.

My husband Abraham is my rock; he was 21 years old and I was 20 when we were married. Some folks thought we were too young to get married and said it would not last. Of course, when we married, we did not consider all the challenges we would experience, especially the ones that came early in our marriage. We did not know how to manage when things happened. But I can tell you it is nothing but the grace of God that allowed us to make it through. The Bible tells us that trials test our perseverance. In the first book of James, who was the half-brother of Jesus, it says *"Consider it pure joy, my brothers and sisters, whenever you face trials of many kinds, because you know that the testing of your faith produces perseverance. Let perseverance finish its work so that you may be mature and complete, not lacking anything."* (James 1:2 - 4 NIV)

Look what God can do! Almost 50 years after our wedding, I often tell Abraham how much I love and appreciate him. He is a godly man who looks beyond my faults and he knows how to forgive. One of the ministers at church told me as others have said to me, "You light up when you talk about your husband." I've cried every time I had to travel without him. And the tears flowed when I returned and saw him standing there waiting for me at the airport. Jeremiah 29:11 NIV says, *"For I know the plans I have for you,' declares the Lord, 'plans to prosper you and not to harm you, plans to give you hope and a future."*

The relationship I have with my husband is not one sided; we also complement each other. I am his helpmate. Genesis 2:18 NIV says *"The LORD God said, 'It is not good for man to be alone. I will make a helper suitable for him.'"* We both must be forgiving, patient and devoted. People tease us and ask, "Where is your other half? When I see one of you, I see the other." Ecclesiastes 4:9-11 NIV says, *"Two are better than one, because they have a good return for their labor: If either of them falls down, one can help the other up. But pity anyone who falls and has no one to help them up. Also, if two lie down together, they will keep warm."*

In 1983, after my mother died, I began to experience severe pain in every joint in my body, requiring me to use a cane or walker to get around. There were periods when the pain became very debilitating. I could not sleep, sometimes I could not do anything on my own. Abraham bathed me and took care of my needs. His actions honor the Bible verse that says, *"Husbands, love your wives, just as Christ loved the church and gave himself up for her."* (Ephesians 5:25 NIV).

Doctors kept telling me they could not find anything wrong with me. To understand what was wrong, I requested that my primary care doctor refer me to a good psychiatrist. I thought my condition was psychological because it started after my mother's death. It took more than two years, several different doctors, and various tests and medications to treat the symptoms. A church sister, Mariam, suggested I see the doctor for whom she worked. After the consultation and a biopsy, Dr. Werner Barth finally diagnosed my conditions.

As a result of the medications I had to take through the years, I developed stomach ulcers and had an eroded esophagus. I also developed pericarditis, which doctors explained is fluid accumulated around my heart. Some of my conditions required me to have several operations. During one of these surgeries, my pressure dropped so low that the surgeon called in additional surgeons, who had to give me a blood transfusion to save my life. Abraham and my dad were in the waiting room praying. You see, we pray to the 'Ultimate Surgeon' before all surgeries. As always, God was keeping me. This is just another reason I praise Him.

I call on Jesus, my Lord and Savior, and praise God for keeping me. And sometimes, it is not with words — it's with tears of joy and gratitude. Psalm 146:1-2 NIV says, *"Praise the LORD. Praise the LORD, my soul. I will praise the LORD all my life; I will sing praise to my God as long as I live."*

NEVER LOSING MY FAITH

By Mary Pollard

*I can't survive without GOD
and His only begotten son, JESUS.*

I realize that since I rededicated my life to Jesus on September 8, 2013 and found a church home at First Baptist Church of Highland Park in Landover, Maryland, the devil got really upset with me and has been pursuing someone who means a lot to me, my daughter.

While at work one day, I received a phone call from 18-year-old Precious, saying that she was being arrested for fighting a bully who had harassed her constantly during the last part of her freshman year at Hillman University. According to our records, the incident was just a "peace order" that was filed and later thrown out by a judge when we went to court. We were not aware or informed that there were two charges related to the fight. My daughter put me on the phone with the arresting officer who was very concerned and polite. I shared the same information with him that my daughter had shared. The officer explained the procedures and told me where they were taking her.

Before I left work in Washington, D.C., I said a prayer. I caught the subway to my car, met my husband and then we drove to Baltimore. While riding the subway, tears flowed. I hummed and sung the hymn, "Come on in the Room" by the Georgia Mass Choir. Now, as my husband and I traveled, I continued to hum and sing that hymn. When we arrived in Baltimore, we were told that our daughter would not be released until she met with the Police Commissioner and/or judge the next morning.

Despite this unsettling news, I kept humming and singing that hymn softly. I asked if I could see my daughter but was told "No." The tears rolled down my face like a faucet, but I still had that hymn on my mind and kept praying and waiting patiently because I asked God to direct me on this. I NEVER, EVER thought that I would have to go through an incident like this.

While waiting at the facility, a female officer came over and said that she noticed I had been there a long time. I had arrived in Baltimore at 5 p.m. and the officer approached me around 10 p.m. The officer asked me for my daughter's name and went to check on her. I said, "Can you please tell her that her parents are waiting?" After about 30 minutes, the officer returned and said that my daughter was fine. I asked, "Are you sure?" The officer replied, "Ma'am, trust me, she's going to be okay." I'm thinking the worse about everything I had heard, read or saw in movies about jails. I thanked the officer and thanked Jesus while that hymn still resonated in my mind.

While riding back home, I continued praying and asking God to protect my daughter from all harm and danger. I continued to pray at home. Early the next morning, the phone rang. When I picked it up, I listened and told the person on the other end, "Okay, I will be down there to pay bail." I cried out "JESUS" because what the police said and what I know God can do didn't add up. My daughter's fight with the bully had been merely a fisticuff. "So, why a bond?" I thought to myself. "She must've really put a whipping on the bully." That's nothing to be proud of, but as a young child, my daughter was picked on and her father taught her how to fight.

When we arrived in Baltimore the second time, we were told that the house that we had been living in for almost 21 years could not be used as collateral for bail and that we needed to contact a bondsman. Still, that hymn flooded my mind. We contacted a bondsman, paid the bail and I told the devil, "You are a liar. Not today!!!" Glory be to God that He made a way for us to get the money, but we had to wait five hours before my daughter would be released. To myself, I said, "You don't know who I belong to and who my Father is." We waited for another two hours and I continued to sing and hum that hymn.

Going back and forth to court over the next six months was a nightmare but not once did I lose my faith because I know that I serve a mighty God!!! This incident was something that I never had experienced before with any of my daughters. My oldest, Pumpkin, soon will turn 37 years old.

Before the incident, I had started taking a class at church titled, "Experiencing God," taught by Deacon Raymond Nobles. It was very strong on my heart to take this class, although there was a conflict with my participation in the church dance ministry that I also was a member of. I wasn't disappointed. The class was awesome and prepared me for the heart-wrenching ordeal with my daughter, which I described as 'a mother's nightmare.' I completed the class on time, despite the distractions.

In November 2017, my daughter's last court date, not only were the charges dismissed, but the prosecutor apologized to her for having to experience this ordeal. In February 2018, we received a letter indicating that her records and fingerprints were expunged. Precious, now 20, is in her third year at Hillman University.

GOD IS GOOD!!! Jesus is my EVERYTHING!!!!!

MY DIAGNOSIS, MY DELIVERANCE, MY DUTY

By Cynthia J. Pope

In the last three years, there were three monumental, life changing events in my life. I call them: My Diagnosis, My Deliverance and My Duty. I learned many lessons during this time, including an awareness of my health, an understanding of my family and friends and the ways they can help. And most importantly, the significance of having faith, belief and a trust in God.

On December 3, 2016, I received a phone call from my doctor. I could tell that he was hesitant about sharing confidential information over the telephone. I immediately became scared and insisted that he give me the results of the numerous tests I had taken. He did. I was diagnosed with cancer. My mind went blank; tears ran, and I dropped to the floor. I was numb.

Although the holidays were near, I followed the advice of specialists who discussed with me the best course of action. I got a second opinion from an oncologist, talked with numerous specialists and endured three biopsies. Chemotherapy and radiology began in January 2017.

Everything was unexpected, leaving me shocked by it all and hesitant to talk with my daughter and other family members, as well as my friends. But, once I realized I could not go through the process alone, I slowly involved the people closest to me. It also was hard for me to believe that I had cancer. As a matter of fact, as I think back, I did not believe it. I went through the motions of chemo and radiation treatments because I understood that was what doctors prescribed for me.

But what I finally, finally, finally realized was it was GOD who made sure that doctors – the scientists - got it right! It was GOD who guided the hands and minds of the receptionists, the aides, the lab technicians, the nurses, the doctors, the specialists, the oncologist Director, and everybody else! It was GOD who guided my mind and my body to react to those scientific diagnoses and prescribed medicines. It was GOD who took care of me 24/7 including the days and nights I was alone. It was HIM who kept my mind intact, knowing that the prescribed medicines may make me think I was losing my mind, focusing on negative thoughts or causing hallucinations. I thought I was okay with my faith in GOD but as I went through this medical journey, I learned that I had a lot more praying to do and a lot more believing in my Master.

My faith journey included medical treatments, CAT and PET scans, laboratory work and test results. They all began to improve. During my scheduled appointments and before the test results were revealed, I remember telling my oncologist that everything was fine and I'm just waiting for him to catch up to God's healing with his scientific findings. After months of consistent results, my oncologist scheduled an appointment with me to discuss them. On September 23, 2017, prior to my scheduled appointment, my doctor called to tell me that all tests were clear and that my body was DISEASE - CANCER-FREE!!! DELIVERED!

PRAISE! PRAISE! PRAISE! SHOUT! SHOUT! SHOUT!

On September 23, 2018, I celebrated my one-year anniversary of being cancer-free. I have so much to be thankful for. From time to time, I hear others around me expressing their medical trials, either one-on-one or in a group setting. My advice is: a) seek medical counsel, b) follow-up, and c) have faith in God. I share my testimony with them, hoping to encourage and inspire them. This is my DUTY!

The most important lesson that I learned was we must have faith, and trust and always believe in God.

MY WARM BLANKET

By Shirley Purnell

In the summer of 1996, I took a bus trip with my daughter Misha and several cousins to Disney World and Universal Studios in Orlando, Florida. We had a wonderful week of fun and fellowship. On the return home, I remembered that my mother, Florence Marshall, had planned a big family reunion for the first Sunday in September, which also was the homecoming celebration for our families' church of origin in Criglersville, Virginia.

The bus from Florida stopped in Fredericksburg, Virginia, about an hour away from where my mom was having the family reunion celebration. Something was tugging on my heart that I needed to get to that reunion. But I rationalized that by the time I got back to Maryland and made the return trip to Virginia, I would miss most of the festivities. I didn't go. My sister Juanita and family members bragged that it was the best celebration we ever had.

Feeling sad that I had missed the opportunity to fellowship with my many family members I had not seen for years, I spoke with my mom and she reassured me that it was not a big deal that I missed the reunion. Two weeks later, my mom died suddenly from a massive heart attack. I was brokenhearted, not only because she passed, but that I didn't have the opportunity to see her, speak with her, hug her or tell her I loved her.

I went early to the funeral home in Orange, Virginia, to view her remains. Alone in the room with the body, I kneeled to pray. In the still silence, I cried and prayed. I spoke of all my regrets and prayed for peace. As I kneeled before the casket, I was engulfed with a warm feeling as though someone had wrapped me in a warm blanket. I felt an immediate sense of the presence of the Lord. It was so comforting that I couldn't believe it. I was relieved of the deep sense of loss and when I walked away, I knew that I was going to be fine. The Lord has promised in His Word, *"I will not leave you comfortless: I will come to you."* (John 14:18 KJV)

I felt the Lord met me in my hour of need and it certainly deepened my faith. Since my youth, I felt a special relationship with the Lord. I was born on Christmas Day and loved the idea of being born on the day we celebrate the Lord's birth. When I was 12 years old, I accepted Jesus Christ as my Lord and Savior. I wish I could say I continued to walk close with the Lord, but I think the pressure of youth and life challenges pulled me in a different direction for many years.

My mother never gave up on me and she told me that one day, I would recognize my need for the Lord's mercy and grace. That day came in 1989, when I renewed my relationship with the Lord and joined First Baptist Church of Highland Park in Landover, Maryland. I believe my mother's prayers carried me until I found my way back to a deeper walk with the Lord.

Over the years, I have had many demonstrations of Jesus' presence and faithfulness. Although I don't have that "warm blanket" feeling often, I know the Lord is with me and watching over me. I know that the Lord answers prayers. If Jesus could walk on water, heal the sick and raise the dead, I know nothing is impossible for Him. Maybe you had a miraculous healing, or survived a horrific accident, or just experienced the presence of God when you needed him most. I know God is real.

I give all praise to the Lord who is my comfort and strength. I have prayed my way through many challenges, with the assurance that God is near and cares for me. I share my faith with others because I want others to experience the grace and mercy of Christ.

"Wait on the LORD: be of good courage, and he shall strengthen thine heart: wait, I say, on the LORD." (Psalm 27:14 KJV)

CREATED TO SING

By Billie S. Richardson

"I can do all things through Christ which strengtheneth me." (Philippians 4:13 KJV)

I accepted Christ as my Lord and Savior while in elementary school in Fayette, Alabama. While I don't remember much of that experience, I do know that my mother, Ruth, played a key role in my Christian development. She served as a pastor of a Methodist church in the area for more than 20 years. However, my God-given gift of creating songs wasn't revealed until I was an adult working for the federal government in Clarksburg, West Virginia.

The lyrics to my first song came in the late 1990s: *God Bless the children everywhere so they won't feel like they are alone.* The song came to me as I realized it touched the heart of people dealing with suicide in their families. I sang those words at a Combined Federal Campaign talent show created by West Virginia employees to raise money for different charities.

After this experience, other words came to me during different times in my life; these songs are dear to me. I sing them a lot, especially when I am driving. The songs let me know I have a struggle and God has promised not to leave me. Maybe God gave me this gift because I was very shy growing up in Alabama with nine siblings, niece Phyllis and cousin Johnny Mack. I would not speak up in school nor take up for myself when I was bullied by other children. I was very skinny and my mother made most of my clothes.

Just me knocking at your door. Your child needs a blessing! Were lyrics I sang to deal with remembrances of a date rape in the early 1960s. After graduating from high school, I invited a guy from Fayette to take me to a prom/dance in the Automotive Building of a vocational school I attended in Tuscaloosa, Alabama. Unfortunately, he took a different route back home. At other times in my life, I struggled financially and endured bouts of loneliness.

Another tailored-made song was *"He came to me, 'my child, keep the faith.'"* I worked for the federal government in Washington, D.C. for 28 years before having to relocate with my job to West Virginia in 1996. My son Brandon was 14 years old. As a single mom caring for a teenage boy, I didn't want to move, and I became mentally, physically, spiritually and financially stressed. I injured my right knee while living in a hotel and later had to have surgery on the knee. I was hospitalized in Morgantown, West Virginia, for 28 days, suffering from a depression disorder that required electric shock treatments. I would lay for hours in the bed in a fetal position, not wanting to do anything. ...*Pain and suffering don't last always* were the words that burst through my lips.

I thank you, thank you for everything you've done for me. I thank you for my son, my son Brandon. He's been good to me. On those cold winter days, he and I were not feeling right. On my bedside, he came to me. He looked after me during that time. He came to me, by my bedside: 'Mama you got to eat, so you won't get weak. Didn't he tell you it would be over one day? I am going out for a while; I'll be back in a while. If you need me, please call. Didn't he tell you pain, and suffering don't last always.' So, I just want to thank you God for everything you've done for us.

I created *When will the hurt inside go away* from my great nephew Maurio's question when his wife died of cancer in her 40s. ...*I don't know. Jesus knows. He knows somebody who knows.*

In March 2004, I was diagnosed with breast cancer and underwent surgery the next month. Thirty-three rounds of radiation treatments followed, and I had to take medicine for the next five years. During that time, job officials would not grant me advanced leave and I had none available of my own. I was donated hours of leave by co-workers. Praise God! While I filed an Equal Employment Opportunity complaint against the agency, I had to drop it because I retired from that agency and returned to the Maryland area. I was forced to file Chapter 7 bankruptcy before leaving West Virginia. To keep the house from going into foreclosure, I changed to a Chapter 13. The bankruptcy was paid off in 2008.

The many struggles in my life helped me produce this song: *I need you to give me the strength to make it through. I just want to see the view. Be in heaven with you.* I have had about 13 surgeries, including breast cancer surgery. During these struggles and burden, I have had support from a few God-sent friends who have been my rock and helped me get through the hurt, pain, anger and sadness. Many of these "angels" I have known for more than 20 years. One family I have known for more than 45 years.

"I don't know Lord, why people say what they say!" sprang from my mind to my lips when my brother who was living with me was suddenly out of work. At the same time, my son Brandon was living in Georgia and needed money to move items out of storage in Ohio. My sister would not help him, not even give him $10 to $20 as I asked. She said she would if she had it.

When my niece Phyllis died in June 2018, the song that came to me said: *We are not perfect. We are not made that way.* I never had a chance to share these lyrics because the funeral services were held at the mortuary, not the church as the family had wanted. The program was already prepared.

"Lord, I am so tired of being tired. But I still need your blessings every day," is another one of my originals. I have been traumatized many more times than this testimony shows. But I have prayed, "God keep me strong" and I tell my son to stay focused, keep the faith, and never, never give up because it will get better. I developed an intense hobby of flea marketing that helped me earn extra income but also kept me from church. Five years ago, I gave up flea marketing on Sundays and later joined First Baptist Church of Highland Park in Landover, Maryland.

I was on the program to sing at our family's Washington Reunion in July 2018. My talents are well known in the family. So, I asked someone to give me a word and a male relative shouted, "love." I began to sing, *Love, love is the greatest thing. God gives you grace.* But what I had prepared beforehand was:

Have you prayed for your families
Today? have you prayed for the world
Today? Did you pray because it's the right
thing to do or did you pray because
You wanted to?

I thank God for my gifts to make and sing songs, which have helped me climb out of many trials, tribulations and struggles. My talents have strengthened me and my faith.

SEEDS OF LIFE

By Denise Richardson

The 2013 winter doldrums were rough for my 92-year-old dad, John Roy Richardson. He couldn't get out of the house and used crutches to move his arthritic legs around. The weather was beginning to change, and I wanted to get him ready for spring.

Every year, I purchased seeds for him to plant. This year, however, to my surprise, he asked, "what are these for?"

I said, "For you to plant." I bought the seeds early to get a head start, so my dad would not have to ask for the seeds or to tell me what kind of seeds he wanted.

"I'm not gonna be here," he said.

"Oh, Daddy! Yes, you are," I said, thinking he was referring to his physical limitations.

My dad's facial expression told a lot, showing confidence when he said: "These are yours."

I have a close relationship with my Lord and Savior Jesus Christ. I fervently believe that if I ask for anything, I know He can do it. So, I prayed a special prayer that night: "Lord this winter has been hard for Daddy. Give him time to get out in the yard to do the things he loves to do and plant his seeds and enjoy sitting in the yard in the sun."

The weather did change, and Daddy was able to plant and water the new seeds I bought.

In his younger days, my dad's family owned a 92-acre farm in Union County, North Carolina. He kept his hands in the dirt, doing what came naturally for him. Even today, I have vivid memories of the walnut, apple and pecan trees perched in front of my grandparent's white house that had a horseshoe driveway for easy entrance and exit. There was a smokehouse, a hog pen and a hen house next to the home, as well as an outhouse behind the back porch. A rooster crowed the first thing in the morning. We picked cotton that was made into bails and later exchanged in town for money.

Like any typical farm, my father grew crops of okra, tomatoes, squash, yams, blackberries, and corn. Pet dogs romped around; ducks and turtles splashed in a nearby pond.

My parents were the first blacks to move into the Fort Dupont community in 1956. At that time, the area was known as Bradbury Heights in Washington, D.C. as Ridge Road ran from the District of Columbia into Maryland. During the day, my dad worked at the U.S. Government Printing Office. After work and at night and on weekends, he drove a cab.

My dad loved his neighborhood, so a favorite pastime was to sit on the front porch in good weather and let the sun-beams soak in. We would sit, laugh and talk, observing the activities and movements of the area. On this day in 2013, however, our conversation turned to death. While I wasn't expecting us to talk about death, I do know there had been many signs that I didn't want to accept and some that I ignored. I didn't want my dad to go; he was all I had left.

My mom, Clara, died in April 2012. My two older brothers, Broadus and Randolph, were deceased. Broadus' daughter died seven days before he did, and his son died from cancer in 2007. Randolph died in 1987 and had one son who died in 2004.

As my dad and I talked on the front porch, he looked worried as he said, "I don't know if you're going to be all right when I'm gone." As in the past, I didn't want to accept the fact that with each passing day, my dad struggled to be strong for me. I then realized I now had to be strong for him.

"I'm leaving you everything," he said. "It's not much, so you'll have to do the rest."

I didn't know what to say but God knew what he needed to hear. I said, "Daddy don't worry about me. When you really, really feel you're ready to go, go ahead. GOD'S GOT ME."

He asked, "Are you sure?"
I said, "I'm sure, sure."

He smiled as I watched his body relax in the rocking chair, a picture of relief. His face no longer had the look of worry. He trusted that I knew, "GOD'S GOT ME."

God enabled my father to plant and water the seeds. But he was not around to see the fruits of his labor. He died in April of that year, the same month, exactly one year after the passing of my mother.

THROUGH IT ALL, I NEVER LOST MY FAITH

By Shirley N. Richardson

According to man, the health issues I have suffered should have killed me long ago. But, being brought up in the church and hearing about God and His Son, Jesus, I knew I was in divine care.

At the age of 11, I had strep throat that was so severe that the doctor made it very clear to my father that I would have died had he not brought me to the hospital that morning in the spring of 1950. Doctors gave me seven shots in each hip and said I only had "a pin-point" passage in my throat from which to breath. Before the hospital trip, my parents thought I had a sore throat and treated the symptoms as such. When I did not get better, my mom suggested that my dad take me to the hospital.

When I was 12 years old, rheumatic fever took over my body and caused my hands to twist backwards. I could not stand on my legs. Again, my parents thought the illness was minor, that my extremities were reacting to cold weather. However, after a week of being ill and not showing signs of improvement, my temperature started to elevate. My mom said to my dad, "we have got to take this girl to the hospital."

That Sunday morning, I was rushed to D.C. General Hospital in the nation's capital, where doctors gave me emergency care. Although the medical staff did not know what was wrong, they knew there was a problem with my heart. While doctors consulted with my parents in the hallway outside of my hospital room, my temperature rose higher than it had been when I was admitted. I began to hallucinate and scream about "pink elephants coming out of the wall to stampede me." Doctors and the nurses answered my cries and because they knew I was in a very bad way, they contacted a top cardiologist who worked in the metropolitan area. Dr. Bernard Walsh was on vacation at the time but agreed to return to the area immediately.

Dr. Walsh diagnosed me with rheumatic heart disease, which brought on the rheumatic fever. During my hospital stay, the doctor discovered that not only did I have a damaged heart valve from the disease, but I had a hole in my heart from birth. I was hospitalized for six months. When I was released, doctors said I had to rest every day. This was hard because I was an active child. But to avoid exhaustion,

I had to eliminate a lot of the activities I had done before my illness. Attacks of rheumatic fever haunted me periodically from the age of 12 to 20.

There were many times when I was young that I became despondent knowing I could not participate in a lot of activities. I remember one day asking, "Why do I have to suffer with rheumatic heart disease?" I realized what I had said and stopped; I thought about others who may have an illness that was worse than what I had. I knew that I had to believe and trust God, that he would bring me through. He did each time I had these dark moments. I've learned over the years to listen to my body, to appreciate the things I can do and not to worry about the things I cannot do. I learned to make chocolate chip cookies, play the piano by ear, and write poetry. I have never given up. I know God is always here.

When I reached my late teens, I had no plans for marriage because I did not want to be a burden to the man I married. However, I did get married in 1957 and had three children. After going through many illnesses as a child, health issues continued to plague me as a young adult and now as a senior citizen. In 2005, I had heart surgery to close the hole in my heart, and in 2012, I had cancer surgery. I have been cancer free for six years. Then, two years later, I had surgery for cervical stenosis. Despite the health issues, God never left me. Through it all, I never lost my faith.

The doctor told my parents that the type of heart condition I have may not allow me to live to see 80 years old. While I do not know if I will live to see 80, I turned 79 years old on November 1, 2018. Today, I have three grandsons and two great grandchildren. God was with me through all my storms, and through it all, I never lost my faith.

I am still blessed. My God has the final say as to how long I have on this earth. He was with me through all the illnesses and I know He is with me now.

GOD CAN GOD WILL

By Shirley N. Richardson

With each tribulation of life's despair,
We can take our trials to God in prayer.
God can carry us through the storm and rain,
He will get us through our heartaches and pain.
God will console us when we're going through the storms,
And He'll embrace us with His powerful arms.
God knows our doubts, He knows our fears,
He can remove all doubts, and wipe away all tears.
We can pour out to God our sufferings in prayer,
God can hear our prayer because He is everywhere.

He is our Father, and if we allow Him,
God will be our guide,
He is the only One who will forever stand by our side.
No matter what we go through,
whether we are a girl, boy, woman or man,
When we pray to God for help,
He will fix it, because God can.

If we believe and trust in God,
He will make everything alright,
He is our Heavenly Father,
and He watches over us day and night.

I'VE LEARNED TO TRUST GOD

By Rev. Valencia D. Richardson

I was diagnosed with cancer of the esophagus in May 2018. I was shocked and dismayed! I immediately felt that I would die. After all, my mom, Helen, and dad, John, both died of lung cancer in 1991 and 2003, respectively. So I thought, "If my work here is done, I will die. But if I still have work to do, I will live." I decided to let the Lord make the call.

The doctors said I had to have chemotherapy and radiation treatments, followed by surgery. Radiation would be every day and chemo once a week for five hours each time. "Wow!" I thought, "How am I going to do this?" That's when my husband of 44 years, Michael, stepped up to the proverbial plate. He said he would be "Driving Miss Daisy." And, that's what he did every day, and every week. God is so good!

Rev. Valencia D. Richardson

November 12, 1952 - January 16, 2019

During this time is when I realized that when we are too weak to carry ourselves, God really will carry us. Some days, I felt like I was floating with no strength of my own; I was being carried by a power greater than myself. At the end of most chemo and radiation treatments, there is a bell that can be rung so everyone will know you have finished your treatments. Near the end of my treatments, I counted down the days when I could finally ring my bell. The bells were loud, and startling, but everyone in the waiting area at Georgetown University Hospital looked up, smiled and clapped. They too looked forward to their day to ring their bell.

With my treatments over, I began preparing for the surgery to remove most of my esophagus. The procedure included connecting my stomach to what was left of my esophagus. Again, my brain had to float through the thought of my stomach being moved into my chest. I survived the surgery. Praise God! My final report from my doctor was that I have no more cancer, it did not spread, and is very unlikely to return. Through it all, I learned to trust in Jesus, and I learned to trust in God, with my whole heart. Learning that has made all the difference in my life and I give my God, All the Glory!!

Now, I know my work here, is not yet done.

FINDING MY VOICE:
My Connection With
The Holy Spirit
By Wanda J. Rogers

"Sing to him, sing praises to him; tell of all his wonderful acts." (Psalm 105:2 NIV)

My earliest memories of my voice and singing go back to when I was four or five years old. I was raised in Pleasantville, New Jersey, a small town in South Jersey where my mother and her two brothers and one sister were all accomplished musicians. My mother, Ella, was better known throughout the area for her beautiful singing voice. She was professionally trained and often was paid to sing at events. Ironically, my father, Harry, couldn't hum a tune.

Mom rehearsed at home when we were young. My three sisters, two brothers and I eagerly sought to accompany her but, my mom would let us know her unhappiness with a loud "shut up." As I listened to her, I learned the songs she sang. My early repertoire included music from Broadway plays, popular movies, and contemporary gospel.

My mom placed me and my siblings in the children's choir at our family church, Calvary Baptist, to manage our desire to sing. Calvary was a very small church that was founded by a group that included my paternal grandmother. Besides the choir, I took on other duties at the church too. I have a unique speaking voice, which always garnered me much attention. However, during choir rehearsals and Sunday services, I would stand in the rear of the choir loft, singing softly because I was insecure and afraid my peers would laugh at my strong vibrato.

As a youngster, I would conduct my own master classes, repeatedly playing the records of Gladys Knight, Diana Ross, Dionne Warwick, and Aretha Franklin. I tirelessly mimicked their vocal styles. As I became more confident, the church choir director would give me small solo parts and my elementary school teacher, Katherine McEachern, did the same. I sang the lead in our sixth-grade version of "The Sound of Music" at Woodland Avenue Elementary School.

When I left home to attend Rider College in Lawrenceville, New Jersey, I continued to dabble in song. Again, I found myself handling my vocal insecurities as I had in elementary and high school, standing in the rear of the college gospel choir. God orchestrated my college solo debut in an interesting way. My roommate, a good singer but better dancer from South Jersey, was asked to sing the Good Witch lead for "The Wiz" but could not because of a cold. She had heard me singing in our dorm room and recommended to the director that I sing the lead.

Nervously, I practiced day and night. When the time came, the theater stage was black except for the spotlight on me in my white dress. I closed my eyes and sang "If You Believe" originally sung by Lena Horne. The verse in that song that has stayed with me for more than 40 years is "believe in yourself, right from the start; believe in the magic that's inside your heart." When the song ended, I opened my eyes to a thunderous standing ovation. I had trusted in the Lord and believed He helped me find my voice.

It was after this experience I learned that singing about love and more specifically, God's love, allowed me to overcome my insecurities and connect with the Holy Spirit. When closing my eyes and opening my mouth, my voice becomes His.

In 2013, I had a health scare that affected my throat. It was during a cold Sunday morning in February while preparing for church that I noticed a huge throbbing lump on my throat. I had to sing solos at two services, so I made the decision to go to church and check on my throat later. I sang my solos and went to urgent care after church. After many tests, it was determined that I had a thyroid polyp that had hemorrhaged. After needles painfully drained fluid from my throat several times over the next few months, I decided to have my thyroid removed. The surgeon said after the operation that everything went well, but I should know that my vocal chords were anatomically incorrect. The doctor explained that my vocal chords were on the wrong side of my throat.

I still sing. I find that the more I use my voice, the stronger it becomes. This is not my doing but it is the gift of God. How marvelous it is for God to take my insecurities and imperfections and make them to His glory!

"You made all the delicate, inner parts of the body
and knit me together in my mother's womb.
Thank you for making me so wonderfully complex!
Your workmanship is marvelous - how well I know it.
You watched me as I was being formed in utter seclusion,
as I woven together in the dark of the womb.
You saw me before I was born.
Every day of my life was recorded in your book.
Every moment was laid out
before a single day had passed.
How precious are your thoughts about me, O God.
They cannot be numbered!
I can't even count them;
they outnumber the grains of sand!
And when I wake up, you are still with me!"

~ Psalm 139: 13-18

Chapter Four

Contributors S through W

"Thank you for making me so wonderfully complex!

Your workmanship is marvelous - how well I know it."

~ Psalm 139:14

STRETCH MARKS FOR YOUR PURPOSE

By Dr. Betty D. Seltzer

Some women during pregnancy develop stretch marks as the baby develops in the womb. The mother's skin stretches to accommodate the growth of the baby. Similarly, as a Christian, we develop as God stretches our faith to allow us to trust Him more and more. This is my story on how the Lord has stretched my faith, particularly during my career.

My career was primarily in human resources where I learned a lot about people and their behaviors. I was blessed to work at six federal agencies; I gained knowledge of various leadership styles that prepared me to become the business owner I am today. As a federal employee, I was shaped and stretched as my faith was tested on numerous occasions. As I gained more seniority, the challenges I experienced increased. When circumstances became intolerable, I prayed, and the Lord opened doors so that I either moved to a new position within the same agency or transferred to another agency with a promotion. The Lord knows how much we can bear. I held management positions and received awards and recognition throughout my career. I believed that God was shaping and preparing me for *greater* based on the challenges I experienced.

For example, I began to receive less than stellar performance ratings, which reduced my awards. I did not complain to my manager about my performance award because I know that everything belongs to God. Instead, I asked and received a revision of the inaccurate description of my performance. I know that what man means for evil that God will turn it around for good. God stretched my faith as I served Him, ran for or with Him. I knew that God was stretching me for *greater.* Can we be direct here? *I KNEW* that my boss and a few co-workers viewed me as a threat and tried to find a way to minimize my ability. I also know that the devil has a way of inserting doubt even when you know that you are doing your best.

In response, I evaluated my attitude and worked to adjust where necessary. I stopped complaining and started praying. There were opportunities that came my way, which my manager did not plan nor foresee. When my boss gave me an intentionally challenging assignment, God prevailed through me. Another example is a time the Lord afforded an opportunity for me to travel out of state with a team of individuals considered experts in the area of human resources

accountability and compliance. When I submitted my "af-
ter-action report," which outlined our findings and recommendations, the document could not be refuted. For some
reason, my manager wanted to test my writing style, although previous managers had complimented my writing
abilities. A God-given gift I possess is the ability to write
and formulate my thoughts on paper. The Lord has a way of
perfecting your gift(s). God will *"do exceedingly abundantly
above all that [you can] ask or think"* (Ephesians 3:20 NKJV),
because you honor Him.

During challenging times, I constantly tell myself that God
is stretching me. I have learned to take a deep breath to get
rid of the toxins. I recite the Scripture, "I can do all things
through Christ which strengtheneth me." (Philippians 4:13
KJV). As I become mature in Christ, I try to worry less and
pray more. God's word says, *"In his kindness God called
you to share in his eternal glory by means of Christ Jesus.
So after you have suffered a little while, he will restore,
support, and strengthen you, and he will place you on a
firm foundation."* (1 Peter 5:10)

When stretching your faith, there may be doubts and uncer-
tainty about completing the task. I *know* that my God will
never leave me nor forsake me. Though I struggle sometimes to rid myself of doubt, I know that I cannot quit during
difficult times and that God is stretching me for a purpose.

Isaiah tells us *"they that wait [on] the Lord shall renew their strength."* (Isaiah 40:31 KJV). I have been stretched beyond my imagination by being allowed to retire early from the federal government and becoming the owner and CEO of Betty Seltzer Insurance Agency. I can honestly say that *God will grant you the desires of your heart if you trust Him and endure to the end.* Trust God to place you on a firm foundation and allow Him to give you stretch marks for His purpose.

TRUST AND OBEY
By Dr. D. Kim Singleton

There was a time when I thought I controlled the directions my life could take. Parents, church family and school taught me to pray, prepare and act. So, from kindergarten through college, I developed Plans A and B to guide me. Crises sprinkled in throughout the years caused me to regroup and follow Plan B but, overall, my ship sailed smoothly across the water.

My life flourished and I continued to work Plan A, earning a doctorate degree, getting my dream jobs and preparing to have a private practice in psychology. As I studied for the license, Mark 11:24 (KJV) echoed in my mind: *"Therefore I say to you, whatever things you ask when you pray, believe that you receive them, and you will have them."* I prayed to pass the examination, followed my Plan A and didn't doubt that the results would be what I wanted. The Board of Psychologist Examiners approved my application and I took the 'Part I' written examination on October 19, 1979.

A month later, on November 27, my smiles faded when I received a letter that I did not pass the examination. Puffy eyes betrayed the tears I shed secretly. Not only did I need the license for a private practice, it also was the first time my Plan A wasn't working and there was no Plan B. The disappointment hurt. "Why?" flooded my conversations with God. At my lowest point, I cried, "Lord, I know you're there but it sure doesn't feel like it right now. Please give me some proof that You are. I know this is a bold request, but I need something concrete. I need to know so I can follow You forever without doubt. If You aren't, I need to know that, too, so I can go my own way." Waiting over the following seven months forced me to reexamine my thoughts and beliefs. I concluded that my request was silly, accepted "what-will-be-will-be" and moved on with new plans.

Then on June 13, 1980, the Board of Psychologist Examiners sent a letter requesting me to appear for the Part II oral interview on June 24. I was confused. The board said I had failed the first part exam. Three days later, I received a letter that explained it all: *"On November 27, 1979 you received a letter from this office advising you that you did not pass the examination of Professional Practice in Psychology. However, I am in receipt of a letter from the Professional Examination Service advising that the initial failure notification was erroneous and in fact you passed the examination. I regret any inconvenience, but the matter was beyond my control."*

I knew this was not a coincidence. I knew it was the concrete answer to my bold prayer request. The board's July 15, 1980 notice advised of my application approval and I received my license to practice psychology effective August 7, 1980. The rest is history. Training enhanced my gift of discernment and prepared me for my mission and ministry as a psychologist. I came to understand that exercising this gift in my life and work fulfills the purpose for which God created me.

Several truths are etched in my memory. While challenges and obstacles have come into my life, I know Christ is the author and finisher of my fate; He has promised never to leave nor forsake me and "Faith" is stepping boldly into the future, even though I don't always know how, when and where it will happen but knowing it will. The Scripture I learned as a child continues to guide me daily: *"Trust in the Lord with all thine heart; and lean not unto thine own understanding. In all thy ways acknowledge Him, and He shall direct thy paths."* (Proverbs 3:5-6 KJV)

A TESTIMONY
FROM THE HEART

By Gene A. Smith

God has been good to me and my family. We have been truly blessed. Daily we thank Him for bringing us through cancer, automobile accidents and all types of surgeries. When trials and tribulations seem to be impossible, He is always on time to solve whatever we are confronted with. I say to all, whatever seems to be that we cannot handle, call on the Lord day and night and keep on keeping on. Most of all, thank Him for saving our souls.

AN ANGEL CAME INTO MY LIFE

By Joanna Smith

We often speak of angels watching over us, even in our songs. But do we ever feel that God puts one directly in our lives to help us get over the hills and through the valleys we are surely going to encounter? I am one who feels His hand in my life.

My husband died in April 1964, leaving me a 35-year-old widow with four children, ages 1, 7, 9 and 10. I was terminated from my U.S. government job at the end of May the same year. I lived in Columbus, Ohio at the time, and 2,000 jobs were transferred from my hometown to St. Louis, Missouri. I felt I couldn't move with the job because my family was in Columbus and could help me raise my children. So, going to St. Louis was out of the question for me.

The Personnel Office in Columbus notified those of us seeking employment that a clerk-typist test was available. I had not typed in years, but I remembered the saying "nothing beats a try but a failure," so I signed up to take the test. When that day arrived, the weather was hot, and the testing area was very cold from the air conditioning. I immediately began to pray to God because, not only were my hands cold but, the typewriters were electric.

The last typewriter I used was the manual type where you had to hit the keys hard to get them to strike the paper on the roller. I took the test and waited a couple of weeks to hear from someone. I called the Personnel Office and was told that I was among the few who passed the test. I remember asking the person I was talking to, "You must have heard I was recently widowed?" But the person did not know me of course. It was then that I realized that God heard my prayer and I rejoiced, knowing He watches over me.

I continued to look for employment as I waited for a job offer from the government. I lived on unemployment checks at that time. Then one day, the Personnel Office called me about a 90-day position at the Lockbourne Air Force Base near Columbus, and asked if I was interested in working for the Comptroller. Of course, I said "Yes," because that was better than going to the unemployment office once a week. I went to the job interview and afterwards waited for the day the job would start. The Personnel Office called me and said the military base wanted them to send someone else because I said I could not type. My response was: "Who would go on a typing interview and say they couldn't type?" The Personnel Office put in the necessary paperwork and said I would be notified when to start the job.

My job was to fill in for the Colonel's secretary who was on maternity leave and I would type financial reports for the Finance Department. After two months on the job, the Colonel called me into his office and said he was being transferred to Biggs Air Force Base, near El Paso, Texas. He wanted to tell me what a pleasure it was to have me working for him. It was at this point that I realized that when I was initially sent to Lockbourne AFB and the Colonel saw on my record that I was recently widowed with four children, he thought I was not up to doing a good job. That was the reason he asked for the Personnel Office to send him someone else. He said he had spoken to the Finance Officer and told him that if I liked working at the base, a job should be created for me when my time was up in his office.

I was given the position of Military Pay Clerk, but never saw a military pay record. I was detailed to the Travel Unit, which handled orders for military travel. One of the airmen requiring advance pay travel was Sgt. Roosevelt Smith Jr., who promised to take me to lunch if he didn't have to wait long when he returned from Texas to clear his travel advance. Roosevelt knew that our office was very busy arranging travel for troops being sent to Vietnam. He did take me to lunch.

During my short time at the military base, I think every young trooper heard I was a recent widow and would try to invite me to lunch. I turned them all down and carried my lunch so that I could eat at my desk and read "The Daily Bread" and my Bible. However, my sorority, Delta Sigma Theta, was having a formal dinner dance and I needed a date. I asked the sergeant I carpooled with if he knew any single airmen on base and he pointed to Sgt. Smith and gave me his phone number. When I called, he was hesitant because he had another job after his military duties were over. Within a week, he called and said he'd made arrangements with his other job and he needed me to give him the particulars of the dance and my address.

On the day of the dinner dance, I threw an after party. My Delta sisters were so impressed with my date because of his mannerisms. He was a gentleman. I had to tell my friends he was just a date. Then, I learned he was eight years younger than me. When the evening was over, he asked if he could come back sometime to meet the children, which he eventually did. Once he met them, especially my youngest, who was 2 ½ years old at the time, he began to come over more frequently and bring them candy and gum. At one point, he said, "You need someone to look after you." I ignored that remark but shortly afterwards, I stayed home with a sinus infection and he called to see why I wasn't at work. When I told him, he said he had orders to go to Idaho and that elevation would be good for my sinuses. I laughed in response.

Within a week after that, he also received orders to go to Vietnam. He seemed confused, so I told him, "Forget about Idaho, you are going to Vietnam." He was told he had a 30-day leave before going to Vietnam. He called me and said, "I want to marry you before I go." I responded, "You don't even know me. I suggest you go home and be with your dad."

Roosevelt eventually went to Fairfield, Alabama, his home, but continued to call me. So, I said to him, "If you make it out of Vietnam, you have a wife."

We courted with recorded letter tapes because he wanted me and the children to talk to him. The courtship lasted for 10 months. Then, he showed up in Oakland, California, called me and gave me two days to join him. He had sent money for the plane flight and wedding rings. I had never flown before then. We were married on October 13, 1966.

This could only happen with God's grace. We had two children together and a wonderful marriage for 39 years. He was called to glory on April 26, 2006. I must believe God sent me an ANGEL. When he said he wanted to marry me, I said, "You must think I have money, since I have a house and car." His response was, "I see your paycheck in Personnel and know you need help."

To God Be the Glory!

WAY MAKER ORCHESTRATED

By Mary E. Smith

One of the most alarming experiences I've ever had happened on a cool fall afternoon in October 2014. I was driving my car South across Interstate 95/495 in the second lane from the right shoulder while returning home to Fort Washington, Maryland from a funeral service at First Baptist Church of Highland Park in Landover. I was singing "There's a Bright Side Somewhere" when my "dependable," 13-year-old Honda Accord, fondly called Black Beauty, suddenly stopped!

I immediately panicked. Several other emotions came upon me, but the worst was fear because vehicles were zooming past my car on both sides at super high speeds, making it impossible for me to get out of my car. Everything I thought I knew to do in emergencies had left my memory and caused temporary paralysis. Bowing my head in total frustration, I simply said, "Lord, help me."

As I reached for my phone to call roadside service and my son-in-law, who is my rescuer for household repairs, I heard a tap on my window. A stranger named Mr. Lewis asked if I was okay and told me, "Hold on, we're going to let you get out." As I looked around to see who the "we" were, I saw a car parked very close behind mine and a man on the outside waving traffic around us. Mr. Lewis helped me get out of my car and walk to the shoulder and I began making my phone calls. He and his passenger moved my car to the shoulder. After accepting my gratitude and refusing the money I offered, they left. Within minutes, emergency responders — police, fire truck, and an ambulance — came. Soon thereafter, my son-in-law arrived.

After examining the car, the mechanic made the determination that I had a transmission problem. My son-in-law immediately said, "Mom, it's time for a new car." My response was, "No way. I've never had any problems with this car, and I cannot afford a car, new or used. There has to be another way." I opted to have Black Beauty towed to my home, instead of a repair shop, where it was parked for several days until I explored all my options. I contacted my automobile insurance company, which sent its mechanic out to my home for further examination. The mechanic also said that the problem was the transmission and made a few suggestions. I was then convinced that though Black Beauty had served me well for such a long time, it was time to let it go.

While realizing that this was the best solution, I also knew that because I maintain a conservative budget, with no funds available for any sizable purchases, the expense of a car, would be financially detrimental for me. For three days, I wrestled with unsure and uncomfortable feelings about purchasing a car. Though I understand that sometimes one must go against the norm to satisfy her needs, I also knew that it would take divine intervention to make this happen.

After all, I am a retired government annuitant with only enough funds for my current needs. Tiring myself from praying, meditating, researching, and making telephone calls, I surrendered, and said, "If this is God's will, it will happen. If not, He will provide another means of transportation." Four days later, Black Beauty was donated and towed away by a charitable organization. My son-in-law drove me to a Honda dealership in Bowie, Maryland where, after spending more than four hours, I drove off the lot in a new car.

Three days later, after all my negative emotions subsided, and feeling relatively calm, I received an unexpected telephone call. It was from a real estate agent, who had worked with me for approximately eight months searching for houses for sale so that I could downsize to a home more suitable for my health challenges than the three-story townhouse I owned. I had cancelled the search when seemingly there were no houses for sale with my specifications. However, this phone call came six months after cancelling the search. Curious and anxious, I listened intently.

Following the pleasantries, I heard, "Ms. Smith, I have a house for you ... true to your specifications. Are you available tomorrow? I'd like for you to see it."

Shocked, but somewhat excited, I said, "What? You've got to be kidding ... NO way can this be happening! I just bought a car four days ago!"

I began to vacillate over this overwhelming news and probability of pursuing it. Very aware of my financial situation, I thought, "Stop this process now before we're at the point of embarrassment."

But I was persuaded to "at least look at the house." My son-in-law and I met there with the agent. As I walked into each room, I tried not to be excited because everything was perfect to my specifications. Internally, my thoughts were, "Don't get excited ...this is too perfect ...you know this will never happen. You've got to sell *your* house, and that's going to take time. What about finances and other known and unknown qualifications?"

I doubted whether there was a need to pray about it because I viewed this request to be absurd. I was not remembering that God loves this kind of request. I tried to dismiss the idea of downsizing, and to make myself satisfied with sitting on the steps of the stairs inside my home, scooting up and down from floor to floor. But then I remembered Philippians 4:6 (NIV), *"Do not be anxious for anything, but in every situation, by prayer and petition, with thanksgiving, present your request to God."*

My home sold within seven weeks; there were no problems with qualifications, and best of all, finances to and from me were ideal to my requirements as well as the purchaser of my home. I moved into my home three years and six months ago.

I have continued to tithe my income just as I have for the past 52 years and have made on-time payments for all my bills with money available to cover expenses and some things that I want. How was I blessed like this? Nothing but God's grace! God was and is my Way Maker. Surrendering to God because I trust and depend on Him was another *lesson learned.*

REMOVING THE *"SPIRIT OF FEAR"* TAKES GOD

By Semora T. Johns Smith

For a long time, I hated myself. There was always a feeling of shame and not truly knowing where I belonged. I loved all my five sisters and four brothers; most of all, I loved my mama and grandma. What I didn't like was the fear that consumed me, and my inability to talk to the people who could give me answers. For decades, I concealed the hatred I harbored for myself until I turned 40 and realized that it was time for me to step out of the fear that was destroying my life. It was time for me to stop frontin' and be real.

There were so many things I was afraid of. Growing up without a father was my first fear. Thinking my father had left me and didn't want me was another fear. I feared talking to my mama about it too. Back in those days, children weren't allowed to express themselves or ask questions. We had to accept what we were told or otherwise be labeled disrespectful.

In addition, whatever answers I received from my brothers, sisters, neighbors and everyone who I ever heard call me a bastard brought yet another fear. I thought that was the worse label to have. I feared I would never be good enough because of that label, bastard. I know my mama, grandma, and siblings loved me, but we were all sailing in the same fearful ship and no one could help me the way I really needed it. I longed to know what it meant to be loved by a man and not just a brother. This was at the core of every decision I made; I accepted abusive relationships as a result. A few times, I thought I would be found dead somewhere — either by the men I couldn't break away from or by my own hand.

I found my strength from the people God placed in my life who showed me love. I became an overachiever with hopes of receiving the type of acknowledgment I felt I'd been missing. It made me feel accomplished, but deep within I was hiding the way I really felt about myself. The pain and dysfunction I saw growing up with my mama's decisions and my siblings' marriages lingered throughout my adult life.

There were moments when I should have celebrated and all I could do was cry. I could not believe that I was good enough for the accolades that were coming my way. God showed me that "hiding" my feelings was feeding the fear. Everything that I was trying to hide was revealed in the worst way. I can only imagine that God meant for some of the bruises to show, so others would ask questions and offer help. I dreaded telling my daughter where my name came from and who my daddy really was. I told people for years that he was dead, because he treated me as if I were dead. However, God changed him and now my father is in my life and a good grandfather to my children.

When I acknowledged my fears and accepted my role in nurturing the fear rather than trusting in God, doors opened for me that helped me navigate a path back to God in the most difficult times of my life. I'm excited to tell my story now and I have been doing so nationally for the past couple of years.

Facing my fears saved my life. Now, I'm working to save others. That little girl I was would be proud of me now.

"For you created my inmost being; you knit me together in my mother's womb. I praise you because I am fearfully and wonderfully made; your works are wonderful, I know that full well. My frame was not hidden from you when I was made in the secret place, when I was woven together in the depths of the earth. Your eyes saw my unformed body; all the days ordained for me were written in your book before one of them came to be. How precious to me are your thoughts, God! How vast is the sum of them! Were I to count them, they would outnumber the grains of sand—when I awake, I am still with you."
(Psalm 139:13-18 NIV)

POEMS OF A PSALMIST

By Zinya Smith

The Favor of God

Lord I thank you so much Father for your love!
I thank you Lord for being there for me.
Oh Lord my redeemer, my keeper, the Lover of my Soul.
The favor of the Mantle upon my life,
That love that only a father can give to his child.
Your protection, Your love that sustains me, wherever I go.
The Favor of God continues to be strong!

Don't Procrastinate

Stop being lazy and waiting on a free ride.
You must activate your potential to bring it in the now.
Don't wait, go forth, keep going, keep pursuing.
Push! Praise! Until Something Happens.
Your destiny of greatness will overtake you.
Seek the Lord your God and His righteousness.
What God has for you it is for you! Rise up!
and never be lazy again!

Now You Know

Knowing is half the battle.
Don't stay there, now you know who you are!
Work toward your potential.
The Lord has given you a mandate!
Don't procrastinate! And Don't delay!
Don't Stop! Go all the way!
You will be glad you did!
Now you know you are special and unique!
Greatness in every sense of the Word!
Search no further! It's been there the whole time!
You were born in your mother's womb.
The negative words that were spoken before from others:
Use them to move pass that to get to where you should be!
Now You Know!

The Blessings of the Lord

The blessings of the Lord are upon me.
Thank You Lord You found me
To give and share your love, grace and mercy,
Never knew what I know now.
To be favored and loved by a God like you.
The wisdom you give.
Oh! What a joy, you bring to me and mine.
Many have doubted what you have done.
I will never doubt You are my mind regulator and
my redeemer and the Lover of my soul.
Oh, What a blessing it is to be in the presence of you, Lord.

WE ARE FAMILY

By Rev. Tracy Graves Stevens

We are family. I am family. These words mean everything to me, but the definition has had various meanings over the course of my life. There was a time, after I was married, that being in a family carried so much weight that the thought almost destroyed my confidence and the hope I had for God's promises in my life.

For background, I met my husband, Garry, in an unexpectant season of my life and in an unexpectant place: a nightclub. I just knew when I met him that he *could* be "the one." I wasn't looking for a potential mate that night, which is why that urging to get to know him better was so unusual. We both learned later, as our courtship progressed, that we both felt the same thing that fateful evening.

In the beginning of our relationship, we did all the things we were taught to do to ensure this relationship was *the* one. We prayed. We fasted. We sought wise counsel and once we both received that "spiritual unction" to go forth, we got married. With that part done, what was next?

That is where things got complicated. Life was good, and our love was good. As we settled into our new life together, equipped with careers and a church we loved, we thought the next stage would happen as naturally as the love we developed from that first sighting. During those early years, my husband and I pursued our new life together with vigor and intention. As God blessed us, we blessed our church and others. We purchased a house that was larger than our parents' homes, which made them delighted beyond belief. Something about our successes made our parents feel like they had done their intended job and we felt good that we could make them proud. Well, as in everything in life, there is always a twist, except this twist was more like a rabbit hole.

Even though our new life was flourishing, the only times we had some anxiety were those awkward family dinners where the inevitable question "When are you going to start a family?" would always come up. It didn't matter where we were, that magical question was everywhere — at church, the family reunion, holiday celebrations — everywhere. We couldn't escape it. The hope of starting a family became a source of frustration the longer the time passed with no results. We started to question, "Did we have enough faith?"

My husband and I come from a long line of faithful servants and prayer warriors. They were praying. We were praying. Everybody was praying. With all this praying going on, we began to question our status as a family since the question to us was always, "*When* are you going to *start* a family?" It was as if we weren't a family without children.

As time went on, we began to avoid attending some events because we didn't want the awkwardness. The annual Mother's Day and Father's Day were just painful. Just like many frustrations in life when things don't work out, you isolate. When you isolate, you also begin to feel like a failure. Our inability to get pregnant began the season of questioning everything: Questioning ourselves and our walk with God. What sin did we do that caused this? We questioned each other: What did *you* do to cause this? And, we questioned God, "Why?"

After many trips to many doctors and more surgeries than I care to name, I had to finally come to grips with the new label for women like me — I was infertile. The thing about the journey of infertility is it is not something you jump up and announce at the Wednesday Night Bible Study. Why is that? We can ask for everything else in life, like healing or a new job. But this journey is largely a silent and somewhat lonely one, especially in the church. To cope, Garry and I leaned fully on each other. We prayed together and cried together.

Thankfully, we had a small village of people around us who we trusted but most times, we felt a sense of pity when we lamented the fact we had no children. So, to save face, we smiled and went along, even as our hearts ached. I felt a sense of inadequacy as a wife to my husband because I could not conceive. For the Bible scholars reading this, that should sound a bit familiar as Sarah was not able to give Abraham a child. Remember, she took matters into her own hands when she offered her handmaid, Hagar, to him to father a child ... or, to *start* a family (Genesis 16).

This journey went on for 10 years. In that time, I became an ordained minister and my husband a deacon. There was no lack of faith in our lives. Well-meaning people would anoint us with oil and let us know they were praying for us. Others would accuse us of not having enough faith and to pray harder. We kept the faith, but I found myself asking, "Hey God, I am not getting any younger so if this blessing is coming, what is the holdup?" In hindsight, I guess that was the *Sarah* spirit within me — laughing at God's promise in Genesis 18:12.

It was during this time that God reminded us both that we're family. We were *a* family. We were a part of His family and as a result, we were not alone (Matthew 19:29). God loved us in so many other areas of our lives that we could only sit back in amazement at how He was moving. We felt foolish complaining about this one blessing. Remember though, God says to cast all your cares upon Him because He cares for you (1 Peter 5:7). So, there is nothing foolish in His eyes about your feelings. As I think about this time of my life, I remember how Garry truly proved His love in making me feel whole and loved. What was there to complain about? We did investigate adoption to expand our family but as we settled into the process, some events occurred that made us realize maybe this was not the path God was choosing for us. So, we trusted God for whatever outcome He intended for us, even if it meant no children. God loved us.

God loves you. God has no limitations on what He can do and hears every prayer you cry out to Him. We learned to accept His outcome for our family because we recognized our family is not defined by how many children we didn't have, but the community of believers He put around us. Garry and I were family but realistically, we were family even before we were joined in marriage. I was a part of God's family. And, as a believer, you are as well. We are all family. What a promise!

Endnote: God did eventually bless us with a beautiful daughter 10 years into our marriage. Just like Sarah and Abraham, our child didn't come quickly or according to any plan that we devised. The interesting thing about infertility is it can still be a reality even after you have a child, so it is still a journey Garry and I walk, but we are content with our little family of three. God knows what He is doing, and we don't feel any less "family" as a result. We are family and if you are reading this, you are family too!

MY STORY

By Rev. Brenda Kaye Thompson

I learned of Jesus Christ through a Lutheran elementary school in Landover Hills, Maryland. In my late 20s, I met and married the person I believed to be the love of my life; the man of my dreams. Our meeting in Brewster, New York, in upstate Putnam County, was like a scene from a great romance movie. The first time my eyes met his I said, "He is the one that I've dreamed of all my life." I just knew he would be my husband.

Sometime after meeting, we decided to leave New York and move to Maryland to plan our wedding. His name was Brian and he was from Largo, Maryland and I'm from neighboring Landover. We were married 19 months later and the ceremony was something that fairy tales are made of. We had a night-time, candlelight wedding on the grounds of the Newton White Mansion in Mitchellville. Hundreds of candles flickered everywhere as about 400 people sat for a formal dinner. High profile politicians attended, and the wedding attracted coverage from *The Afro American* newspaper.

About five months after the ceremony, our beautiful baby girl was born. I could not have been happier. However, the happiness ended six days after giving birth because I learned that my closest girlfriend, who had been my roommate for two years in New York, also had given birth to a boy fathered by my husband. This was when my faith and resolution were tested.

I was devastated and dismayed. I couldn't believe that God had allowed this to happen to me. I prayed and fasted, went to pastoral counseling, marriage counseling, and anything else that was suggested. I believed that God would bless my marriage to Brian with mercy, grace, favor and forgiveness. Sadly, that did not happen. Instead, I became despondent and fell into depression.

In college, I had dabbled with illegal substances. Now, with my depression, I returned to what I believed would take away the unbearable pain of betrayal, deceit and dishonesty. Before my marriage, I spent two years in rehabilitation and was delivered from addiction. But now, the pain of betrayal and knowledge of the child outside of our marriage sent me over the edge. I returned to what I knew would relieve the unbelievable pain that I'd just been dealt. I made a conscious decision to start using drugs again. I eventually lost everything, including my marriage, child, and myself. Most importantly, my connection to God had been severed.

I was in a very dark place for about 15 years. During that time, I experienced some horrific things that often accompanies a lifestyle of using and selling drugs. There is a saying that addiction guarantees one of three things: jail, an institution, or death. I experienced them all. The death was definitely spiritual because I felt as if my prayers were hitting the ceiling and that God had totally forsaken and abandoned me.

My spiritual awakening came when God called my mother home. With her death, I felt as if the bottom of my life had fallen out from under me because she was the only person left in my corner. Fewer than 100 days after her death, I returned to federal prison for the fourth time because I did not report to my parole officer. I entered the penal system for what would eventually be my last time. When I awoke on the second day of incarceration, I realized the destruction that I had caused and how it had overtaken me.

I finally, totally surrendered to the only one I knew could help me — God. Just as the prodigal son in the Bible ran home, I ran back to my Father's loving arms. I got on my knees next to my prison bunk and started earnestly praying out loud. Before I knew what was happening, a deep gut-wrenching cry was unleashed that attracted nearby correctional officers who found me taken over by the Spirit of God. My prayer that God would take my desire for drugs away from me and restore me to my right mind was answered.

Before my release from prison more than a year later, God had done a work in me and spoke clearly to me that this entire experience was to bring Him glory. He placed in my spirit a greater desire to learn more and more about Him and to make sure that I tell everyone I met about Jesus and what He'd done for a wretch like me. I made a clear decision to trust Him and to follow His way by first giving Him *all* of my hurt, pain, guilt, and shame. He created in me a clean heart and has truly renewed a right spirit within me.

I have been thriving ever since. There have been some struggles. During much of this time, I had not been in my daughter's life and to this day, she wants nothing to do with me. No matter how much I have apologized, explained, prayed, and cried, her resolve is to act as if I do not exist. That is an unbearable pain to experience. Yet, I know and believe that God is able to restore my one and only child. I know that He controls everything!!

I have known since my late 20s that God was calling me to ministry. However, I had done everything contrary to His will. Much like Jonah in the Bible, I ran in the opposite direction. At that time, I believed that I had gone too far away from Him for Him to still want to use me, but on October 22, 2013, I publicly acknowledged my call to ministry and was licensed to preach the gospel on June 20, 2018. I look forward to God using me wherever He sees fit.

BREAST CANCER DIAGNOSIS
By Lena Thompson

I am a breast cancer survivor and a thriver. I was diagnosed with breast cancer on April 13, 2005, at the age of 52.

I began getting annual mammograms at the age of 30 because of my family's history with cancer. One of my older sisters, Rosa, succumbed to breast cancer on October 19, 1984 at the age of 40. My father, Benjamin H. Williams, died of cancer of the esophagus less than two months later, on December 16, 1984. And, my best girlfriend, Wendi, whom I had known since elementary school, fell victim to breast cancer on August 29, 2003, at the age of 51.

The August before the deaths of my sister and father, my mother, Jannie L. Williams, became sick and was rushed to the hospital with pneumonia. At that time, my dad's cancer had been diagnosed and my sister had undergone a mastectomy. I remember clearly that it was a Friday night and my husband wanted to leave after visiting hours to go home and rest. We got the call in the middle of the night that my mother had died. There I was. My mother was gone, and my dad and sister knew they were terminal. By the end of the year, I had experienced three deaths in six months.

Two months before my diagnosis, on February 11, 2005, I had my annual mammogram. But, a few days later, the X-ray department at the Clinton Medical Center notified me that they found an abnormality and recommended a sonogram to confirm the findings. I scheduled my sonogram for March 7, 2005, when the doctor confirmed there was a lump that needed to be removed. It so happened that this also would be the day of the home-going service for my late sister's 42-year-old son who had died of a brain aneurysm. Talk about timing; it made me think even more about just how precious and short life is. I was battling other issues as well and with all of this, the awakening came that I needed to do something different. I needed to find my way back to Christ; and during this time, I *did* find my way back to Him.

My gynecologist referred me to a surgeon and on April 6, 2005, I underwent a lumpectomy. A week later at my appointment, my husband, Michael, was with me when the surgeon said that cancer was found in the lump that was removed. I'm not sure of anything that she said to me other than the fact that the lump was small, and she wanted to perform a sentinel node biopsy to make sure that the cancer had not spread to my lymph nodes. I shut down and immediately began to think about my sister, my best friend, and all the other women I had known who had succumbed to breast cancer. I wondered how I would tell my son and daughter; Michael also had three children in our blended family. My daughter, the youngest of our children, was away at Clark-Atlanta University and I knew she would want to come home to be with me. Four of my seven siblings were left, and I am the baby in our family. I didn't want to worry anyone. I thank God for my husband, who was able to carry on the conversation with the surgeon, ask questions and then later share that information with me. Michael's faith and strength to remain calm helped me to stay positive and to trust God for His daily provisions.

It took me nearly two days to finally come to my senses. I thought back to the Sunday prior to that doctor's appointment and one of the things that the Rev. Dr. Henry P. Davis III, my pastor at First Baptist Church of Highland Park in Landover, Maryland said during his sermon rang in my mind: "No test, no testimony." I was not going to die just because others had, God assured me. This was another opportunity for me to be a blessing to others just by telling my story. In my family, I felt the responsibility to urge members to get tested early. I remembered whose I was and how God had kept me during some very tumultuous times in my life. Surely, this was not a death diagnosis.

God is so GOOD!! The sentinel node biopsy showed that the cancer had not spread. Doctors said my treatment would consist of six cycles of chemotherapy and 30 radiation treatments. I decided that if I was going to pass this "test," I had to find out all I could about this cancer. My doctors — the surgeon, chemo and radiation oncologists — were wonderful. They all took the time to talk with me and Michael, answer our questions, listen to our concerns, and suggest reading materials. I still made the effort to visit the library for more information.

While at the library, I found an excellent book, "Understanding Lumpectomy — A Treatment Guide for Breast Cancer," by Rosalind Benedet, N.P. and Mark C. Rounsaville, M.D. The book is written in plain English and included all the terms and language that my doctor used. I found it to be very helpful, so much so, that I told my surgeon about it and she has since added it to the list of suggested reading materials for her breast cancer patients.

Even though I was warned about the side effects of both treatments, I was determined that this thing would not be a negative experience for me. I was told that I would lose my hair somewhere around the third chemo treatment. I didn't accept that truth until the day I asked my husband to cut my hair. I had been wearing my hair in twists and was beginning to look ridiculous. Through my tears, I joked with my husband that my head looked like the parting of the Red Sea with the bald scalp that was showing and the twists hanging on in certain spots by thin strands of hair. My husband consoled me by reminding me that my hair would grow back, and the most important thing was that the cancer cells were being killed.

My chemo treatments were administered pretty much on schedule, with minor delays attributed to a low white blood count. It was very frustrating having to give myself shots for the two weeks leading up to the next chemo treatment and praying that my white blood count numbers would be high enough for me to receive the next treatment. We had planned a cruise to the Western Caribbean with 22 family members and friends prior to my diagnosis.

I was to have my last radiation treatment on that Friday before leaving on the cruise the following Wednesday, November 9, 2005. I was concerned that my energy level would be very low, but I was determined to be on that cruise with my family and friends. Well, we made the cruise and had a very memorable time. I was on this cruise, still with no hair and looking sickly, but it was a good testimony to the family. Thank God for His mercy, favor and grace. He worked it out.

Looking back now, I must admit that the few side effects I experienced were very minor, such as mouth sores, acute sensitivity to smells with a burning sensation in the nostrils, and a distaste for cheesecake. This dessert I once loved, now disgusts me. My Christian walk and faith in God have been strengthened through this ordeal. This test has proven to be a blessing to me and my family. We now have a deeper appreciation for life and know the power of prayer. God is keeping me!!

It's now 13 years later and I am still cancer free. I'm still running for Jesus, doing as much as I can, while I can, for as long as I can. I'm grateful to God for brand new mercies. There's plenty to do, I can't stop now.

I now have personalized license plates on my car "No Test." I'm often asked what it means, for example, "Are you a teacher?" To which I explain, "If you don't have a test, you don't have a testimony." But for the grace of God, I HAVE A TESTIMONY!!

VISIONS

By Lunette Warner

I have wanted to tell this story for many years but never had the courage. Few people know that I am a stroke survivor. I work in rehabilitation as a therapist and those patients of mine who suffered a stroke say they feel lost, alone, and scared. I feel blessed to share my experience with them and, in some way, help them in the healing process.

I was 31 years old working as a therapist in the Washington, D.C. metropolitan area when I suddenly started to have the most mind-blowing headaches. They were so painful that I could not focus, I struggled with blurred vision and moments of no sight at all. I was diagnosed with ocular migraines. My doctor taught me how to inject Fiorinal, a barbiturate used in the treatment of headaches, into my thigh. I would give myself two injections a day but found very little relief.

During this time in 1995, I had a casual relationship with the Lord. I would read a few Bible Scriptures from Psalms and the brief messages from "Our Daily Bread." I attended Full Gospel AME Church in Temple Hills, Maryland. You could say I was "working on it."

After three months of the treatment regime for the migraines, I was awakened in the middle of the night with the worse headache I had ever had. The left side of my body was numb, and I had very little vision. I was able to call my mother who lived in the District of Columbia, and she came to my home in Camp Springs, Maryland. She took me to what was then known as Greater Southeast Hospital's Emergency Room. Doctors immediately ordered a spinal tap, thinking that I had meningitis based on the severity of my pain. The test was negative. Over the next three to four days, I underwent a series of tests, including CT scans and drug testing. They all were negative.

The hospital's neurologist suggested that I see a psychiatrist. Since all the tests revealed no abnormalities, it must be in my mind, they thought. Angry, scared and worried, I left the hospital and stayed with my mother temporarily. Although no one knew the source of the *problem*, I was prescribed medications to treat the *symptoms*.

A very close friend recommended another neurologist I had worked with in the past. He was an excellent doctor, one whom I admired, respected and more importantly, trusted. He ordered an MRI. While I was inside the MRI tube, the technician asked me how I was feeling. I told him I had a headache. He said to me, "I guess you do. I just spoke with your doctor and he wants to see you right away." All types of thoughts went through my head. Maybe I had a brain tumor or even cancer, I thought. I was so scared.

I arrived at my doctor's office and they took me back immediately. While sitting on the examination table, my doctor gently placed his hands on my knees and told me that I had a cerebral hemorrhage. I heard what he said but it didn't register in my mind. Then he spelled it out for me: "You had a stroke." I was dumbfounded but at least now I had an answer. He prescribed a "cocktail" of medications to dry up the bleeding in my brain. After eight months, I was slowly weaned off the medications. Within a year, I was completely off all the medications and headache free.

My faith grew stronger with every single day that I could open my eyes and see. God showed me his love. He revealed to me who my real friends were. I knew that my prayers had been answered. I wasn't completely recovered and my endurance was still low. I knew with God's grace, I would return to my old self.

Meanwhile, my mother started a prayer circle at Mt. Olive Baptist Church, our church in Washington, D.C. I was told to read the following verses; all are in the Holman Christian Standard Bible (HCSB) translation:

"The Lord is the One who will go before you. He will be with you; He will not leave you or forsake you. Do not be afraid or discouraged." (Deuteronomy 31:8 - loneliness)

"Do not fear, for I am with you; do not be afraid, for I am your God. I will strengthen you, I will help you; I will hold onto you with My righteous right hand." (Isaiah 41:10 - fear)

"For God has not given us a spirit of fearfulness, but one of power, love and sound judgment." (2 Timothy 1:7 - fear)

"Casting all your cares on Him, because He cares about you." (1 Peter 5:7 - worry)

I cannot express enough the joy and blessing that I feel every day when I wake up and can see. Five years after that harrowing experience, I accepted Jesus Christ as my Lord and Savior!

Halleluiah! Praise God!

WHEN GOD SPEAKS, LISTEN!

By Dottie Waters

On Saturday, October 6, 2012, I had just gotten out of the bathtub when God spoke to me and said, *"you're going to have a stroke."* I immediately called to my niece and said, "Lori, call 911 and tell them that I had a stroke."

That warning from God merely reinforced a deep and abiding relationship I have with my Lord and Savior, Jesus Christ. At that point, I had been walking and talking to the Lord for about 29 years. My walk started in 1983 when I decided to attend church after the death of my 3-month-old son, whom I loved dearly. I changed from a partying girl to someone who began to seek Christ with her whole heart and study His Word. I began to praise God for who He was and that pain that I carried around for years after the death of my son was gone. So, on that Saturday in October, when God spoke, I listened.

I was weak at the time because I was battling the flu. I asked my niece to help me put on my clothes and walk down the stairs. When I reached the eleventh of the 14 steps going down, I had the stroke. The paramedics were soon at my front door, ready to take care of me. I live near Southern Maryland Medical Center in Clinton, Maryland, but the paramedics said the facility was not taking any more patients by ambulance. The only trip they could make, the paramedic said to me, was to the Fort Washington Medical Center.

As God would have it, my husband, Oscar, pulled into the driveway in the middle of the discussion of where to go. The paramedic said that the Southern Maryland Medical Center is a specialty hospital for stroke victims and suggested that they put me into his car and let him take me to Clinton. By this time, I could no longer walk. They placed me in the car and my husband rushed to Southern Maryland. When we arrived, I told hospital staff that I had the flu and I just had a stroke. The doctor examined me and ordered a CAT scan, but it came back negative; no stroke. Next, hospital officials assigned me to a room and said that I needed my eyes examined by an ophthalmologist and my right hand and wrist checked by a neurologist.

I stayed in the hospital for a day and a half. While lying in bed, I felt someone touch me. I looked, and no one was in the room with me. I felt the touch again, but that time God was in my ear saying, "I've got you." I said, "What?" He said again, "I've got you." I did not know what He meant at that time but later I fully understood. The doctor released me from Southern Maryland on Monday, October 8. When I got home, I went to bed, and my body was feeling funny, as if it could float or rise like a balloon with helium in it. I said to my husband three days later, on Thursday evening, that when we got up the next morning, we are going to Washington Hospital Center (WHC) because something is wrong with my body.

On Friday, October 12, 2012, my husband took me to the WHC Emergency Room. I told the nurse and the doctor about everything that had been happening to me. They scheduled another CAT scan and did not see anything. But, when they used the MRI machine, they saw the stroke. The first thing that the nurse said to me was you are so lucky, and I responded, "No ma'am, I'm blessed." It had been six days since I had the stroke and the medical community says that the first 90 minutes of a stroke are crucial. After two weeks of hospitalization, I was released to begin outpatient therapy.

When I started therapy at the rehab facility, I saw patients with deformed faces or twisted facial features. Some walked dragging a leg and or foot; others could not walk at all. I walked in with a mild weakness on my right side that most people could not detect. I'm praising my Savior all day long! HE IS A KEEPER!

KNOWING THE BLESSINGS OF GOD

By Barbara "BJ" Williams

My testimony is about how God worked miracles in my life and continues to do so. Hallelujah! Praise God!! When I was around 6 years old, I asked my grandmother, "Mudder," for permission to be baptized. Mittie B. Battle, "Mudder," was very religious, so my brother, Norman, and I grew up attending St. James Baptist Church in Rocky Mount, North Carolina. It seemed that I knew about God and His goodness from birth. You see, Mudder raised us because my mother was an alcoholic and was unable to care for us.

When I was 9 years old, through God's mercy, my mother stopped drinking and we eventually became close. Miracle One. My mother was diagnosed with cancer in 1950 and doctors gave her six months to live. Again, with God's grace and mercy, my mother lived 21 years until 1971. Miracle Two. That's when I really knew that God sends miracles to those who believe in Him.

So, when I was first diagnosed with cancer in 1978, I found comfort. I was living in Washington, D.C. at the time, working at the Bureau of Engraving and Printing. Many of my best friends, co-workers, and traveling partners smoked. I didn't smoke and had no idea about the dangers of "second-hand smoke" that we now are warned about. I had my right breast removed at that time and survived. Miracle Three. Four years later, in 1982, the cancer returned in my left breast, forcing a second mastectomy. I am still here. Miracle Four.

By this time, I had three children — Lisa, Renee, and Regina. While I was confident based on my earlier experiences, I still had to lean on my faith. My entire focus was for survival and taking care of my children. I am now 77 years old and have also survived two open-heart surgeries in the early 2000s. Miracles Five, Six, and Seven. I thank God daily for His grace and mercy.

My youngest daughter, Regina, has stage four colon cancer, so my prayers are for a healing in her life. I know that His will shall be done. God is a miracle worker and has performed so many in my life. Miracles Eight and Nine came when Regina travelled to Japan to visit her son in the U.S. Army. Despite her weakened condition, she made it through the 20-hour flight going and the 17-hours coming back. God truly is a miracle worker.

I just want to spread the word to anyone who does not know God that He is a good God and worthy to be praised.

To God be the glory!

THIS IS THE LORDS DOING

By Susan Williams

"Delight thyself also in the LORD: and he shall give thee the desires of thine heart." (Psalm 37:4 KJV)

I always wanted to live in the Towers at Westchester Park. The Towers, a high-rise condominium community surrounded by Greenbelt National Park, located in College Park, Maryland. I began thinking seriously about living at the Towers when my long-time friend, Connie, moved there in 1999. She knew I was looking to purchase a home and encouraged me to consider the place where I've always wanted to live. I had looked at different condominiums around Prince George's County in Maryland but none, in my opinion, measured up to the benefits of living at the Towers — well-laid out floor plans, great amenities, good security features, prime location, and of course, Connie. The problem was that the units sold quickly, often the same day they were put on the market. I prayed that God would allow me to purchase a unit there. In fact, throughout my search, I depended on God's guidance, which I've learned to do over the years as I matured in my walk with Him. I believed that if it was His will for me to live there, then I would.

Meanwhile, I continued looking and eventually put a contract on a unit in a condominium community in Hyattsville, Maryland though in my heart, I really wanted to be at the Towers. I can't explain it, but I had a feeling this place in Hyattsville was not for me. I did not feel content with the contract, but I left it in the Lord's hands. As it turned out, the ratio of owner to renter occupancy for this condominium community did not meet the mortgage lender's loan requirements. This was a blessing in disguise, I now realize.

In 2003, Connie, who is a realtor, told me about a unit at the Towers that was in probate. She offered to do all she could to help me purchase it when the deceased owner's heir decided to sell. When I moved into the unit in April 2004, I felt God had answered my prayers. Years later, reflecting on how I felt when I was finally living where I always wanted to live, a verse from one of my favorite Psalms came to mind, *"This is the LORD's doing; it is marvelous in our eyes."* (Psalm 118:23 KJV)

ACKNOWLEDGEMENTS

I honor You, dear Lord. You are the Most High God. I am immensely grateful to You for providing the vision, guidance, and resources for *Joyfully In His Care, Women Living In All Circumstances*. This book stands as evidence of Your steadfast faithfulness towards all who would eventually come together, and play a part in completing Your plan for this book of testimonies.

I thank you, Dr. Henry P. Davis III, beloved pastor of FBHP, for your spiritual leadership, guidance, and trust that the Project HerStory book of testimonies would reap a bountiful harvest in the Kingdom of God. The revered line "If you build it, they will come" from the movie *Field of Dreams* comes to mind when I reflect on your belief that the women would come through with their inspiring and uplifting stories. Project HerStory and *Joyfully In His Care, Women Living In All Circumstances* exist because of your early endorsement.

To the Women's Ministry Coordination Team at the First Baptist Church of Highland Park (FBHP) — Rev. Renee Alston; Sandra Brennan, Minister in Training; First Lady Weptanomah Davis; Eunice Dawkins, Church Clerk; Rev. Dr. Yvonne Felton; and Rev. Tuwana Johnson — I owe you a debt of gratitude for supporting the Project HerStory team in creating the first evangelistic publication of this type to be sponsored by FBHP.

To the extraordinary authors featured in this book, collectively referred to as Women of Faith by the Project HerStory team, I must once again express my never-ending appreciation for each of you. As contributing authors, you and your testimonies make this book an invaluable resource for anyone in need of hope, inspiration, joy, peace, and strength while pressing through life's many challenges. Truly your stories glorify God and declare His enduring love for His people.

Deacon Yvonne Lowe, I repeat words of gratitude to you for immediately seeing and believing in the need for a book of testimonies from the hearts of women in the FBHP community and other faith-based circles. I will always appreciate your work behind the scenes ensuring the project "dotted the I's and crossed the T's." Your acceptance of the unexpected task to create the manuscript for the book truly touched my heart. Without your unwavering faithfulness to Project HerStory, this book of testimonies would have experienced still another setback. I will always treasure our partnership in the many endeavors undertaken for the spiritual growth and development of women. You are a gift from God. There is so much more He plans to reveal to those with willing and open hearts.

To Chief Editor, Dr. Tamara Henry and the editing team — Rev. Tracy Graves Stevens; Bridgette A. Greer, Esq.; Cynthia Roscoe; and Dr. D. Kim Singleton, your help and commitment are undeniable. Thank you for eagerly dedicating the hours necessary for producing a solid work product that served as the foundation for *Joyfully In His Care, Women Living In All Circumstances.* I value the transforming care and attention you gave to each testimony. You made sure each writer's voice was heard, and her individual experience was captured.

To the extraordinary authors featured in this book, collectively referred to as Women of Faith by the Project HerStory team, I must once again express my never-ending appreciation for each of you. As contributing authors, you and your testimonies make this book an invaluable resource for anyone in need of hope, inspiration, joy, peace, and strength while pressing through life's many challenges. Truly your stories glorify God and declare His enduring love for His people.

To Margaret Bamiduro, Nancy Clark, Natashia Hagans, Tiffany Henry, Beverly Johnson, Taneya Pair, and Audrey Wyatt, I thank you for your invaluable support and willingness to serve during and beyond the solicitation of testimonies.

To the "Connections on the Hill" team, budget mastermind Barbara Davis, FBHP Administrative office (Shontta Boyd, Denise Harrison, Deacon Cheryl Logan, and Natalie Powell), Media Ministry (Trustee Joel Price), Photography Ministry (Linda Sims, Deacon Ollie Williams), and the Web Ministry (Deacon Walden Woods), thank you for your individual expertise, service, cooperation, patience, gifts, and talents in assisting and supporting the Project HerStory team in its efforts to meet ever-pressing deadlines.

To Jacqueline Alston, a life friend and spiritual sister since childhood, and Dr. Donald Warner, a prolific author and early supporter of the Project HerStory effort, thank you for your research and recommendations on publishers.

To our legal advisers, Judge Wendy Cartwright, Rosalyn Pugh, Esq., and Niky Woods, Esq., thank you for blessing Project HerStory with your expertise in providing legally sound advice and judgment.

To anyone whose name I did not mention, I extend much gratitude to you. Please know I do not take for granted the time, talent, and resources contributed by you and countless others rooting for the success of this project.

Last but not least, to the beloved and sustaining helpmates of the Project HerStory team, Trustee James Henry, Deacon Alvin Lowe, Brother John L. Scruggs, Brother Garry Stevens, and Trustee Leon Walker, my words are inadequate for expressing love and appreciation to God for placing you in the lives of the Project HerStory team and for being "silent partners" during completion of this book of testimonies. I applaud you as men of God, with gratitude, respect, and love for your accommodating spirits. To God be the glory!

~ Rev. Goldie Walker

ABOUT THE CONTRIBUTORS

Victorine O. Adams, born and raised in Baltimore, Maryland, is the youngest of ten children. She gets her name from an aunt who was the first black woman on the Baltimore City Council. She has three children and three grandchildren. Victorine is a proud member of First Baptist Church of Highland Park where she is a member of the Praise Power Dance Ministry as well as a graduate of the Crown Financial Ministry; all while attending Prince George's Community College.

Cynthia F. Alexander is a member of the First Baptist Church of Highland Park. She describes herself as a mother, grandmother, daughter, child of Christ, retired government worker, and former employee of the Martin Luther King Library in Washington, D.C.

Shirley K. Ballard is retired from public and private sectors after 48 years of an outstanding career. Ten of her years were spent working at the White House under four different presidents. Shirley is busy at the First Baptist Church of Highland Park, serving in several ministries. In her leisure time, she volunteers at Capital Caring Hospice in Landover, Maryland. Shirley, a wife and mother, lends support to her family and friends as needed.

Tonya Barbee, M.B.A., is a bestselling author, inspirational speaker, radio host at WBGR, and project manager. She is founder of I am Still a Rose (IASAR, LLC), an organization that empowers and inspires women to move beyond their past hurts and find happiness within themselves in spite of it all. She is the single mother of four children and has seven grandchildren. Tonya resides in Bowie, Maryland.

Sidonie A. Becton, Esq., is a native Washingtonian, avid reader, creative writer, and sports enthusiast. She is also a proud member of Delta Sigma Theta Sorority, Incorporated. Sidonie is a licensed attorney maintaining a practice in intellectual property, sports and entertainment law.

Rev. Yasmin Bell-Flemons is completing her Ph.D. in Higher Education Administration at Liberty University in Lynchburg, Virginia. For the past decade she has been employed by the Department of the Navy, United States Marine Corps as a Certified Program Trainer. A native New Yorker from the village of Harlem, Yasmin has contributed innumerable volunteer hours to the Multiple Sclerosis Society.

Catherine T. Bennett retired from the federal government on January 3, 2019 after serving 50 years of service. Catherine's last 22 years were with the Department of Justice, Office of the Attorney General. She has been married for 41 years and has two children and one grandchild.

Janice L Boone has been a faithful and dedicated member of the First Baptist Church of Highland Park since 1995. She is blessed with four wonderfully talented, inspiring, gifted children: Karla, Sharon, Darrell, and Christopher. With her former military family, she travelled the world; and was blessed to reside in Albuquerque, New Mexico; Bremerhaven, Germany; and to spend several months in France. She enjoys her duties and responsibilities as a talented and resourceful member of the Media Ministry. In addition, she relishes the Greeter Ministry where she often greets members and visitors coming into the house of God to worship the Lord.

Joann Antoinette Borges-Palmer is a Minister-In-Training at the First Baptist Church of Highland Park and currently is embarking on a new chapter in her life as she walks with her Lord and Savior, Jesus Christ. Joann believes that together we can make a difference when we serve. Joann says to the Lord, "I'm ready. You showed me Your grace, now my life's renewed and I thank you!"

Joyce Brooks is a third generation Washingtonian who loves the District of Columbia. Joyce is a Crime Prevention Specialist for the Howard University Department of Public Safety. In this capacity she utilizes her *people skills* daily. Above all else, Joyce loves the Lord!

Ironia M. Broyles is a long-term member of the First Baptist Church of Highland Park (FBHP). Ironia is a part of the Prison Ministry, the AWANA Ministry, and the Gospel Tract

Ministry. To enhance her Christian growth, she is a member of the FBHP Sunday Biblical Institute women's class. Currently, she is also enrolled in the International Bible Study Fellowship classes.

Wanda Cartwright is a long-standing member of the First Baptist Church of Highland Park. She has, over the years, served her church as a member of the Library and Discipleship ministries. Wanda works for the Library of Congress but in her personal time she loves to read books as well as book reviews, and to write.

Wendy A. Cartwright is a member of the First Baptist Church of Highland Park where she has served as a young adult usher, a member of the Trustee Ministry, and Co-Chair of the Building Committee. Judge Cartwright has been appointed and elected as Chief Judge of the Orphans' Court for Prince George's County, Maryland since 2003. Since 1991, Judge Cartwright has maintained a private practice, Cartwright & White, LLC, which primarily consists of cases in family law.

Robin Cashwell is an information technology consultant who has a Bachelor of Science degree in Computer Information Systems. Robin has been ministering in prisons since completing biblical and foundational studies at the Spirit of Faith Bible Institute in 2009. She is now a Minister-In-Training at the First Baptist Church of Highland Park, answering the call of God in her life to fulfill His purpose. Robin has two adult children and one grandson.

Deacon Joyce E. Chandler is a native Washingtonian and the second oldest of three children. Joyce is retired from the Metropolitan Police Department of the District of Columbia after a thirty-five-year career. She is the mother of two boys and one spiritual daughter and the proud grandmother of 14 grandchildren and 6 great-grandchildren. She serves as a deacon, evangelist, and President of the January Birthday Ministry at the First Baptist Church of Highland Park (FBHP). Also, Joyce participates in visiting the sick and shut-in through the FBHP Benevolence Ministry.

Audrey Chase is a native Washingtonian who currently resides with her husband, Dr. K. Bernard Chase, in Upper Marlboro, Maryland. Audrey is the mother of three adult children and the grandmother of five. It is no secret that singing God's praises brings her sheer joy and definition to all aspects of her life's journey.

Dorothy Simpson Cotton has been a member of First Baptist Church of Highland Park for more than 44 years, joining the church as Rev. James C. Wyatt handed the baton to the Rev. Dr. James J. McCord. She was working in the church office periodically when the Rev. Dr. Henry P. Davis III arrived and grew her responsibilities to include welcoming new members, working with wedding couples and praying by phone with those who requested it. She also was president of the February Birthday Fellowship and a member of the Outreach/Inreach Ministry.

Rev. Janie M. Crawford was born in Lawrence County, South Carolina. She attended public schools in Washington. D.C., graduating from Cardozo High School. She attended the National Academy of Music and sang around the city, in various venues and churches, for many years. One noted performance was singing on the same program as noted singer Leontyne Price. Rev. Crawford retired from the Smithsonian Institution in 1981 after 35 years of service. An ordained minister, she received her calling to preach in 1981. She furthered her theological studies at Howard University, receiving a master's degree in religion. Rev. Crawford joined First Baptist Church of Highland Park (FBHP) in 2011, where she serves as an associate minister. Rev. Crawford was married to the late Russell W. Crawford, Sr. She has one son and daughter-in-law, FBHP Deacons Russell W. Crawford, Jr. and Cheryl Crawford, three grandchildren, and four great-grandchildren. Rev. Crawford's favorite Scripture is Psalm 91 and her favorite song is "Precious Lord."

Sandra Edmonds Crewe, **M.S.W., Ph.D., ACSW**, is Dean of the Howard University School of Social Work and a National Association of Social Workers (NASW) Social Work Pioneer ©. She has been a social worker for more than 40 years beginning her career in the unchartered areas of public and assisted housing. Dr. Crewe, a native of Halifax County, Virginia, was among the wave of young African Americans in the mid-1960s who desegregated high schools in the state. She feels that this painful exposure to the cruel and lasting damaging effects of structural inequalities at the age of 14 informed her decision to become a social worker with a focus on eradicating inequities. She has dedicated her career and life to improving the quality of life for underserved and marginalized populations. Dr. Crewe has authored more than 70 publications focused on social justice, caregiving, aging among African Americans, social isolation, and welfare reform. She has received numerous awards. Dr. Crewe resides in Largo, Maryland with her husband, Dwight. They have two sons, Dwight and Paul. She is a 40+ year member of First Baptist Church of Highland Park.

Barbara M. Davis is a retired manager of strategic planning for an information technology firm. Barbara uses her talents, gained in the private sector, to help a non-profit organization seek grant funds that will help people who are victims of crime. Barbara serves on her church's budget committee. Also, she has spent many years on the Board of Directors of two credit unions.

Rev. Costella H. Davis is a gifted singer and writer of plays and skits with Christian values. Costella served as an associate minister at the First Baptist Church of Highland Park and now serves in a church planting season with her sisters. She resides in Mitchellville, Maryland and is the mother of an amazing daughter, Abbie.

Chekesha M. Duncan has a special name — Chekesha is Swahili for 'gift of laughter'. She is truly living her name as she believes the joy of the Lord is her strength.

Carolyn M. Ellerbe credits her outlook on life to an upbringing with godly parents, early life experiences with overcoming adversity, and her current loving family. Her mother was born bound in peonage, a form of twentieth-century slavery in the South and endured a hard life. Her father, a free man, was her mother's savior. Despite the hardships and difficulties in their lives, Carolyn's parents knew and loved the Lord and taught their children godly values. They taught their children to praise God for His grace and mercy and to forgive those who abused them. Carolyn eventually gained an understanding of this type of forgiveness. Her peace, hope, and joy came when she knew God for herself.

Today, Carolyn wants her light to shine so others may see God in her. She studies God's Word and thanks Him for where He brought her from and the path she is on now. She is a retiree of the U.S. Government Printing Office (GPO). She loves decorating and organizing spaces; creating center pieces and floral arrangements; helping others in need; donating her time and talent at her church; and traveling. She resides in Upper Marlboro, Maryland with her loving husband. They have two sons.

Sharon Everett-Hardin is an outgoing person who loves to read, go to Broadway plays, and spend time with family and friends. An avid runner, Sharon has participated in several races - specifically the Army 10 Miler (2015-2017), the Marine Corp 10k (2016-2017), Black and Missing 5k (2016-2017), and Pancreatic Cancer 5k (2016-2017). She is a past

President of the First Baptist Church of Highland Park September Birthday Ministry and is currently the ministry's Recording Secretary. She has also worked with the Women's Retreat Ministry.

Robin Fields loves the Lord and knows Him as her Lord and Savior. As a member of First Baptist Church of Highland Park she worships at midweek services on Wednesdays as well as on the weekends. She dances for the Lord whenever the opportunity is presented. In her spare time, Robin enjoys bowling and playing pool.

Candice C. Floyd has been in love with words before she could read. When Candice isn't reading, she spends her days at Prince George's Community College in the library and her evenings and Saturday's teaching students to also love words through her English Composition courses. She currently resides in Fort Washington, Maryland with her husband and their son.

Destiny "Des" Floyd is a First Baptist Church of Highland Park teenager. She is self-motivated and loves serving the Lord as an active member of the Junior Missionary Ministry, Sunday Biblical Institute, and Evangelism Ministry. Destiny loves travelling. As a 2019 high school graduate with honors, her education continues as a freshman student at Salisbury State College, Salisbury, Maryland.

Jennifer Floyd is a dedicated member of First Baptist Church of Highland Park. She heads up the Missionary Ministry and expounds its goals to reach the needs of others globally and domestically.

Odessa Burnette Gatewood is a member of Penn Avenue Missionary Baptist Church located in Oxford, North Carolina. Odessa is a retired employee of the North Carolina Department of Public Safety. Odessa previously served in capacities of probation-parole officer, day reporting center officer, cognitive behavior intervention trainer and instructor, chief probation-parole officer, assistant judicial district manager, and judicial district manager. She has and is currently working contractually in related capacities. Her interests and hobbies beyond work are varied — word games and crossword puzzles, poetry composition, Metro-Goldwyn-Mayer films, Transatlantic/African Slave Trade and Slave Voyages research, vintage shopping, group exercising, family socials, and more.

Betty Bunns Gay resides in Mitchellville, Maryland. Betty is the mother of two daughters and a son, and God has blessed her with two lovely granddaughters.

Rev. Joyce Gray-Thomas is a retired branch chief from the U.S. Department of Energy. Joyce received her bachelor's degree from American University and her master's degree from Maple Springs Baptist College and Seminary. She has been a facilitator for courses offered through the

Discipleship Ministry at First Baptist Church of Highland Park for over 12 years and is also actively involved in the Evangelism Ministry. Joyce is married and has five grandchildren.

Bridgette Ann Greer, Esq. is a native of Plainfield, New Jersey and has lived in Prince George's County, Maryland since 1988. She is an attorney and has worked for the Prince George's County Government for over thirty years. In her spare time, Bridgette enjoys exercising, reading, volunteering, mentoring, and advocating the importance of organ donation.

Natashia Hagans is an early childhood educator, a disciple for Christ, and an inspiring writer and poet who believes in empowering humans with the gift of spoken word.

Deacon Shirley A. Harper retired as a supervisor from the Federal Bureau of Investigation after 37 years of service. She, along with her husband, served as church coordinator of the Crown Financial Ministries at the First Baptist Church of Highland Park for 22 years. Shirley and her husband have three children, two grandsons, and eight great-grandchildren. Shirley enjoys texting encouraging, spirit-filled notes to her family all over the country.

Alicia Hawkins is a procurement manager for an international non-profit organization in Washington, D.C. Alicia came to this country at the age of 15 from San Salvador and is a dedicated mother, wife, daughter, friend, and survivor.

She and her husband of 15 years have two teenagers, a daughter and son, and reside in Upper Marlboro, Maryland.

Inez Henderson is a retired educator from the Prince George's County Public School system in Maryland. She sees her story as a continuation of what she tried to do in her professional career working with students from kindergarten through high school as a servant of God. She is married to a wonderful man and is the proud mother of three young adults and five grandchildren.

Aravia Holloman is a soon-to-be retired analyst with the Environmental Protection Agency. She calls herself a "country girl", who loves to read, cook, and travel. A strong believer in education, Aravia has tutored and taught mathematics.

Tanya E. Hood, a native of Washington, D.C., is a wife, mother, and business owner. She is avid about her faith and trusts in God in all activities because without His grace and power she knows she could do nothing. Her goal is to not only have a positive effect on herself and her family but also to inspire, motivate, and create lasting change in everyone she encounters.

Denise Branch Jackson is a wife of 30 years and the mother of two adult children. A self-titled information junkie, Denise is also an avid gardener.

Rev. Nicole S. Jalloh, a federal government administrator, is also a licensed minister and relentless advocate for civil rights, equality, and justice, specifically serving Moms Demand Action for Gun Sense in America. Rev. Jalloh is an associate minister on the ministerial staff at the First Baptist Church of Highland Park.

Beverly R. Johnson is an assistant controller for an environmental justice and policy shaping non-profit organization. Beverly is a devoted mother, an avid reader, an occasional writer, and singer. She loves to find artistic outlets to express herself. When Beverly is not serving in various ministries at church, she can be found traveling with her job or spending time with her family.

Brittany C. Johnson is a local singer and teacher. She uses her love for music to minister to and encourage people of all ages. Brittany is also the founder of OnStage Performing Arts Collective, LLC, where young people come to hone their artistic skills and build their love for the arts.

Dawn N. Johnson is a mentor, writer, reader and active facilitator. She is known for her compassionate spirit and willingness to serve others. She loves spending time with friends and family and is also a proud mother to her beautiful daughter, Destiny Johnson.

Kayla Johnson is a 21-year-old Caribbean American woman pursuing a degree in nursing from Prince George's Community College in Largo, Maryland. Kayla has a final goal to become a nurse practitioner and open her own private practice, in the South, for single mothers and underprivileged teenagers. Kayla has a passion to guide and improve the lives of others, hence her love for nursing. She is currently working as a geriatric and certified nursing assistant throughout the Washington D.C. metropolitan area.

Shirley Johnson, a widow, is retired from the U.S. Department of Education after 33 years of service. She is a proud member of First Baptist Church of Highland Park serving in the choir and other ministries. Shirley volunteers for the Prince George's County Department of Permits, Inspection and Enforcement where she reviews applications filed by various building contractors and homeowners seeking licenses and waivers.

Femi Kay is the only female child of Cherokee and Cameroonian parents. Femi was born and raised in the nation's capital and now resides in Florida *by the Bay*. She and her two adult sons spread joy, culture, consciousness, and love throughout the world; artistically drawing on numerous high energy talents and gifts bestowed upon them by God.

Vernell Lawson is an executive assistant to the president of Bowie State University. Prior to this appointment, Vernell served as assistant to the chair of Prince George's County in the Maryland General Assembly, House of Delegates, in Annapolis, Maryland.

Rev. Dr. Patricia H. Love is a native of Bucksport, South Carolina where she grew up and attended the Salem African Methodist Episcopal Church. Currently, she is a minister of the Altar International Church. Dr. Love traveled to Malawi, Africa in July 2018 for mission work in the kingdom of God and that was a life changing mission for her. Dr. Love and her husband reside in New Carrollton, Maryland. They are the proud parents of three loving children.

Dorothy Marks-Fontenot has been happily married to Rev. Dr. Albert E. Fontenot, Jr. for the past 13 years. They have five children and lovingly call themselves "the Brady Bunch." They also have 21 grandchildren. Dorothy retired from Chicago Public Schools after 37 years as a certified school nurse. She holds a bachelor's degree from the Loyola University of Chicago and a Master of Education from Concordia University in River Forest, Illinois. She continued her education and received certificates that allowed her to be one of the lead nurses for the westside area of Chicago.

Presently, Dorothy devotes her time to trying to be the best usher she can be at the First Baptist Church of Highland Park. She and her husband are also part of the Marriage Ministry and Guidance Ministry. They co-facilitate Hope Reborn (DivorceCare) on Sunday mornings.

Susan A. McLaughlin is a retiree from the Federal Bureau of Investigations. She puts God and family first, which has helped her navigate her fight with breast cancer and minister to others in their struggles. She is a wife, grandmother, and bright light to everyone she meets. Susan's glass is always half-full.

Theresa M.T. Melton ("Terecka"), has worked for more than three decades as an issue-expert in marketing, media relations and strategic communications. She has been performing and entertaining audiences professionally for over ten years. Her favorite Scripture is Jeremiah 29:11, "For I know the plans I have for you, declares the Lord. Plans to prosper you and not to harm you. Plans to give you a hope and a future." Theresa has been married to Julius A. Melton for 27 years and they reside in Clinton, Maryland.

Elizabeth Newburn is a cancer survivor. She is an advocate for other cancer survivors and for celebrating life. Elizabeth, a retired healthcare worker, has served in many area hospitals including Doctors Hospital of Washington, D.C., Children's National Hospital, and Providence Hospital.

Wanda Leigh Offley is retired from the District of Columbia Public Schools after 23 years of service. She is also part owner of Tastefully Divine Catering Company. Wanda is the mother of one son and the grandmother of three amazing grandchildren.

Kathryn P. Osborne has been a native of Prince George's County, Maryland for 60 years. She is a graduate of the Prince Georges County School system and the Prince George's

Community College. She is a writer, the visionary and founder of K. Scott Gallery and Cultural Center, and G.L.O.W. in the Spirit Women's Gathering.

Taneya Pair, a Washington, D.C. native, is an active member of the First Baptist Church of Highland Park and other non-profit organizations. Taneya has a master's degree in Mental Health Counseling from Trinity Washington University and is also a co-author of the book titled *Share Your Testimony: Vol. 1 Women Who Overcome*.

Laverne A. Parks is a great-grandmother who is devoted to her family and has a passion for service. Laverne likes nurturing youth and caring for seniors. She is a retired Equal Employment Opportunity (EEO) practitioner with over 39 years of federal government service. It was there she was known as the "Hat Lady." Laverne attended Antioch Law School Center for Legal Studies in Washington, D.C. and the Duke University Law School, Private Adjudication Center. She is also a national public speaker, trainer/facilitator, mediator, and Certified Notary Signing Agent.

Laverne has served on the executive boards of the Federally Employed Women (FEW), the National Federal Women's Interagency Counsel (FWPIC), Prince George's County Habitat for Humanity, the Speaker Bureau (now known as the Fuller Center for Housing in Prince George's County), the Southeast Crisis Pregnancy Center of Washington, D.C., and Teenarama, Incorporated.

Mary Pollard is a praise dancer for the First Baptist Church of Highland Park Praise Power Dance Ministry and enjoys her contribution to this unique ministry. She is also a volunteer bus driver at the church. Mary is the proud mother of two children and the grandmother of four.

Cynthia J. Pope is retired from a financial institute and enjoys reading, journaling, raising plants and flowers, traveling, socializing with friends, volunteering, and going to church. She does part-time work and has three outstanding grandchildren.

Shirley Purnell is a retired federal human resources manager. She is the mother of one adult daughter. She enjoys God's Word and serves as a substitute Sunday School teacher. Shirley enjoys reading and her favorite hobby is designing and making jewelry.

Billie Sue Richardson is a retired federal government supervisor from the Department of Justice. She has one son and three grandchildren. Billie is from Fayette, Alabama and is a member of the First Baptist Church of Highland Park family.

Denise Richardson is a retired addiction counselor, presently working as a caregiver in the Gerontology Department at the University of the District of Columbia. Denise is also a jewelry instructor at her neighborhood community center and loves her commitment to the Tuesday Night Prayer Line. She is a native Washingtonian and cherishes spending time with family, especially her grandchildren, Jennie and Sydney.

Shirley N. Richardson studied Social Science and Human Societies at the University of the District of Columbia. Shirley worked for the Federal Government for 28 years and retired in December 1999. She is the mother of four children, with one twin transitioning in 1996, the grandmother of three grandsons, and great-grandmother of two. Shirley is a homemaker and likes to write poetry.

Rev. Valencia Richardson (The testimony "I've Learned to Trust God!" was published posthumously for Valencia D. Richardson): Valencia was a registered nurse, certified bereavement counselor, and licensed reverend at her home church, First Baptist Church of Highland Park. She loved nursing, working in the operating room, and helping people cope with their losses. Her book, *No More Pain*, was a roadmap to showing how she received her healing. Valencia was a wife for 45 years to her childhood sweetheart, mother of 2 adult children, and grandmother to 5 grandchildren at the time of her transition.

Wanda J. Rogers is a retired federal executive and entrepreneur. She is an active member of the Fine Arts Ministry at First Baptist Church of Highland Park and serves as the chairperson of a local non-profit that services the residents of Prince George's County, Maryland. A member of Delta Sigma Theta Sorority Incorporated, Wanda and her husband, Terry, reside in Bowie, Maryland. They both enjoy traveling as well as spending their free time with their adult children and grandchildren.

Dr. Betty Ritter Seltzer is an author, a professional speaker, and a business owner/CEO specializing in business insurance, disability insurance, life insurance, annuities, and bonds. She has been a licensed insurance agent since 2005. Betty conducts presentations for businesses and is a student mentor and partner at local high schools. She holds a Doctor of Philosophy in Business Administration from Northcentral University. Her dissertation, published in 2009, is titled *Exploring How Spirituality Shapes Workplace Ethical Perceptions Among African America Women*. Betty is a native New Yorker, a wife, and mother of three awesome sons.

Dr. D. Kim Singleton is a licensed clinical psychologist and author. Kim is a graduate of Howard University and George Washington University located in Washington, D.C. She is a member of First Baptist Church of Highland Park and a proud member of Alpha Kappa Alpha Sorority, Inc.

Gene Audrey Smith is a native of King George County, Virginia. Gene has three children, six grandchildren, and four great-grandchildren. Her career includes employment with PepsiCo, the U.S. Department of Commerce, and the U.S. Department of Justice where she worked in various capacities. She earned certificates from CPT Computer College and Secretarial Business College. In her spare time, Gene enjoys reading and making floral arrangements. She is a member the First Baptist Church of Highland Park.

Joanna Smith is a retired accounting supervisor at the U.S. Department of Health and Human Services. She likes to spend her time at church and with her sorority, Delta Sigma Theta, Incorporated.

Mary E. Smith retired from the government as a management analyst for the Department of Finance and Revenue located in Washington, D.C. She is the published playwright of *Spiritual Plays for Christmas, Easter, and Other Occasions.* Much pleasure comes to Mary from spending time with her family of one daughter, three grandchildren, and one great-grandson.

Semora T. Johns Smith is the lead program manager for one of the world's largest scientific organizations. She is also the Associate Director of the Music and Arts Ministry of First Baptist Church of Highland Park. Of note, Semora was a semi-finalist in the 2016 World Championship of Public Speaking with her speech "Fear Didn't Ruin me, It Saved Me." Semora is the mother of two beautiful daughters, which she considers her greatest achievement.

Zinya Smith is a native of Washington, D.C. She is the mother of two and a grandmother. A graduate of Anacostia High School, Zinya supports her community as an activist for children's education through mentoring. She has a bachelor's degree in business administration from Ashworth College. She is also a licensed minister, graduating with honors from New Life Hope Seminary School, with a theological and divinity degree.

Zinya is a credentialed counselor with the American Association of Christian Counselors; an author of the book titled *This Too Shall Pass*, which is a compilation of inspirational stories of life's trials and triumphs; a talk show host on the WBGR Network, hosting *The Javii and Zinya Show*; and the executive acquisition director for the WBGR Shopping Network.

Rev. Tracy Graves Stevens is a chief experience officer, leadership advisor, ordained minister, and author of the book *What Just Happened? Living the Redeemed Life When All Hell Breaks Loose.* Tracy has a heart for ministering to others through the broken times of life and inspires all through her blog "Living the Redeemed Life". Her favorite verse is *"... nothing [is] impossible with God"* (Luke 1:37 NASB).

Rev. Brenda Kaye Thompson is proud to share her journey from the pits to the pulpit. She is passionate about sharing the gospel message of God's redeeming love with the incarcerated and those re-entering society. Brenda believes that you should never give up on anyone because miracles happen every day. Her estranged relationship with her daughter puts her in the posture to wait on the Lord who has renewed her strength to continue forward – Faith Strong!

Lena Thompson is a retired federal government public relations officer, homemaker, and an available grandmother/great-grandmother (better known as E-Ma). She enjoys spending time with her husband and family, traveling, listening to music, line dancing, and serving Christ.

Lunette Warner, a graduate of Harvard University and Drexel University in rehabilitation medicine, specializes in women's health. She currently attends Zion Church in Landover, Maryland. She enjoys cooking and spending time with friends and family.

Dorothy Treasea Waters, a native of Washington, D.C., has been living in Prince George's County, Maryland since 1981. She has been married to Oscar Waters III for 42 years and is the mother of Oscar Waters IV (deceased) and Shadawn Waters. Dorothy is the grandmother of three adorable granddaughters: Nadia, Autumn, and Aidan. She enjoys writing poetry and hopes to publish a book in the near future. Dorothy loves walking with the Lord daily and is grateful for all that He has done in her life.

Barbara "BJ" Williams is a long-time member of the First Baptist Church of Highland Park. She carries out her calling to sing to the glory of God as an active and committed member of the Fine Arts and Music Ministry. She is a warm and loving mother of three daughters (Lisa, Renee, and Regina), eight grandchildren and sixteen great-grandchildren.

Susan Williams is a native of Louisville, Kentucky. She is retired from the District of Columbia Department of Health after 44 years of service as a licensed practical nurse (LPN). Susan believes in helping where help is needed and is a volunteer at the First Baptist Church of Highland Park's Seasoned Saints Center and the Wellness Ministry. Susan has one son, "Big Will", three grandchildren, and four great-grandchildren.

Women Of Faith

Seated Row (left to right): Taneya Pair, Semora Johns Smith, Wanda J. Rogers, Shirley A. Harper, Mary E. Smith, Cynthia F. Alexander, Rev. Janie M. Crawford, Alicia M. Hawkins, Joyce Chandler, Rev. Brenda K. Thompson.

Row 2 (left to right): Dawn J. Johnson, Cynthia J. Pope, Joyce Brooks, Inez Henderson, Sidonie Becton, Susan A McLaughlin, Catherine T. Bennett, Dorothy Waters, Shirley Johnson, Candice C. Floyd, Tanya E. Hood, Joann A. Borges-Palmer, Barbara M. Davis, Theresa M.T. Melton, Wanda Cartwright.

Row 3 (left to right): Rev. Nicole Jalloh, Lena M. Thompson, Joanna Smith, Audrey B. Chase, Shirley Ballard, Tracy Stevens, Denise Jackson, Susan Williams, Ironia Broyles, Kathryn Osborne, Robin Cashwell, Mary L. Pollard, Rev. Joyce Gray-Thomas, Yasmine Bell-Flemons, Natashia Hagans, Laverne Parks, Betty Gay, Wendy Cartwright.

Women Of Faith

Seated Row (left to right): Shirley Purnell, Gene A. Smith, Sharon Everett-Hardin, Dr. Betty D. Seltzer, Aravia L. Holloman, Rev. Costella H. Davis, Rev. Dr. Patricia H. Love, Denise Richardson, Shirley Richardson, Elizabeth Newburn.

Back Row (left to right): Vernell Lawson, Tonya Barbee, Carolyn Ellerbe, Janice L. Boone, Dorothy Marks-Fontenot, Bridgette Ann Greer, Esq., Zinya Smith.

Women Of Faith

Seated Row (left to right): Lunette Warner; Dr. D. Kim Singleton; Dr. Sandra Edmonds Crewe.

Back Row (left to right): Robin Fields; Billie S. Richardson; Barbara "BJ" Williams.

Women Of Faith

Dorothy Simpson Cotton

Wanda Leigh Offley

Victorine Adams

Inez Henderson

Kayla Johnson

Beverly Johnson

Women Of Faith

Brittany Johnson

Jennifer & Destiny Floyd

Odessa Gatewood

Femi Kay

Chekesha Duncan

What others are saying about *Joyfully In His Care: Women Living In All Circumstances*...

"Many times in our life's journey we have feelings of self-doubt, despair and depression all the while understanding we are blessed. This juxtaposition can lead us to isolate. "Joyfully In His Care: Women Living In All Circumstances" helps us realize we are not alone, and God is always with us. Thank you to the visionary, the collaborators and authors for unselfishly sharing. Know that you have helped someone along the way and your/our living is not in vain." **~ Andrea C. Harrison, Maryland House of Delegates, 24th District**

"I sincerely and wholeheartedly endorse Joyfully In His Care: Women Living In All Circumstances. As you read the testimonies you will know and feel without a doubt that God is real and is always there for you just as He continues to be with these Women of Faith." **~ Cereta Lee, Elected Register of Wills and Member of Maryland Association of Judges of the Orphans Court, Prince George's County**

"Joyfully In His Care: Women Living In All Circumstances is a must read full of transparent testimonials from women who have experienced God and allowed the light of God's Word to shape and build their trust in Him." **~ Jennifer Silver, Licensed Graduate Professional Counselor**